LAW FORUM SERIES
College of Law, Ohio State University

REFORM OF COURT
RULE-MAKING PROCEDURES

REFORM OF COURT
RULE-MAKING PROCEDURES

JACK B. WEINSTEIN

Ohio State University Press
Columbus, Ohio
1977

Manufactured in the United States of America

Library of Congress Cataloging in Publication Data

Weinstein, Jack B
    Reform of court rule-making procedures.

    (Law forum series)
    1. Court rules—United States. I. Title.
II. Series.
KF8734.W43   347'.73'5   77-8391
ISBN 0-8142-0280-2

CONTENTS

PREFACE

ANY LARGE INSTITUTION has the problem of governing itself and of regulating its own procedures. The organizational pattern can often be analogized to that of governments. Big business, the church, and universities obviously fall into such patterns. Internally there are functions that can be characterized as judicial, legislative, and executive.

What we sometimes lose sight of is that organs of government are themselves somewhat independent units, particularly under our theory of separation of powers, requiring internal controls and procedures that replicate executive, legislative, and judicial forms. The presidency and federal legislature have been so thoroughly studied that these internal organizational patterns are widely appreciated. What is not generally recognized, even among judges, is that the federal judicial system is itself a huge and complex organization with thousands of employees and a budget of hundreds of millions of dollars. Our state judicial systems are often even more complex.

For reasons partly beyond the scope of this volume, the judges themselves generally control the judicial establishment. In addition to deciding cases they therefore have assumed many nonadjudicative functions. For example, district judges appoint clerks of the court and thus run a large bureaucracy indirectly; they appoint probation officers and control some of their policies (and this branch of my own district court has some one hundred members); they appoint many subjudges such as magistrates and bankruptcy judges; and they assign work within the courts.

Much of this internal work has only recently come under study as the need for specially trained court executives has been recognized. Some practices now need reconsideration. It is not inappropriate to ask questions such as the following: Should subjudges be appointed, as in the past, by judges on the basis of their own knowledge of the bar with some informal consultations outside the court, or should a formalized merit selection plan be adopted? Are the rudimentary budgeting and planning techniques of the past satisfactory in providing an adequate judicial structure?

In the course of my work as a teacher, judge, and member of many bar associations and judicial committees I have begun to consider some of these issues. It is my hope to be able to develop my ideas on them in the future in a somewhat systematic way.

In this volume I have addressed myself to one aspect of the legislative nonadjudicatory function of the judiciary—rule-making. Rules adopted by and for courts can be of great significance to the way the system operates. For example, Rule 23 of the Federal Rules of Civil Procedure, dealing with class actions, was amended by the Supreme Court on recommendation of supporting committees with no public hearings and almost no debate. The rule has had an enormous influence in encouraging suits in environmental, consumer, securities, and civil rights matters. In contrast to the *in camera* procedures

Preface

utilized in adopting federal class-actions rules, when the New York legislature addressed itself to the same problems, public debate ranged over a number of years, and the legislation was treated as a major reform requiring editorials by news media and public positions by political candidates and lobbying groups.

My purpose in writing this volume is not to consider the merits of class actions or of any other procedural detail. I have had more than my say on these subjects in books, articles, and opinions. What is of primary concern here is the *process* by which rules of procedure are adopted by the courts. This aspect of the nonadjudicative work of judges does affect the public welfare and is therefore worthy of study. For me, however, it is particularly interesting because it shows the unique blend of theory and practicality that makes the American system work. Such concepts as separation of powers or the rule against advisory opinions yield to the need to govern effectively. Yet, principle and theory remain viable, imposing substantial restraints on expediency.

Were it not for the graciousness of the faculty and students of the Law School of Ohio State University in inviting me to discuss these problems with them, and the deadlines they wisely set, none of this would have been written. I am grateful for the assistance of William Bonvillian of the Connecticut and Washington, D.C., bars, for his assistance, particularly in developing the historical discussion. Denise Cote and Keith Secular, both of the New York bar, have assisted in gathering material and making editorial suggestions. Dorothy Rosenberg assumed some added clerical duties. The errors are my own.

Jack B. Weinstein

Great Neck, N.Y.
April, 1976

ADDENDUM

DEVELOPMENTS in the field of rule-making continue at a rapid pace. Some of them are described in an article in the Columbia Law Review sent to the press some months after these lectures were completed. *See* Weinstein, *Revision of Federal Rulemaking Process,* 76 Colum L. Rev. 905 (1976). *See* also Weinstein, *Reform of the Federal Rule-making Process,* 77 A.B.A.J. 47 (1977).

Within the last few months our court has drafted proposed local rules for magistrates pursuant to congressional permission (28 U.S.C. § 636(b)(4), P.L. 94-577, 90 Stat. 2729 (1976)); has adopted substantial changes in its "plan" respecting selection of jurors (28 U.S.C. § 1863) and in its local bankruptcy rules (Rules of Bankruptcy Procedures, Rule 927); and has extensively revised our forms for habeas corpus petitions (Rules Governing Section 2254 and 2255 Cases in the Federal Courts, eff. Feb. 1, 1977, P.L. 94-426, 95-577 [1976]). The public was not involved in these activities. We have also considered proposed changes in the Federal Rules of Criminal Procedure giving appellate courts the right to review sentences—a rule I strongly oppose on the ground that a statute is required, although I do favor both appellate review of sentences and adoption of sentencing guidelines. *See* 76 Colum. L. Rev. *op. cit., supra* at nn. 171-73. Moreover, the stream of directives, suggestions and forms from various sources in Washington and elsewhere, seeking to improve practice, continues to increase. *See id.* at nn. 278-79 (uniform federal rules of disciplinary enforcement),

In their fine 1977 text on Judicial Administration, Russell R. Wheeler of the National Center for State Courts and Howard R. Whitcomb of Lehigh University address themselves to the following techniques for improving the administration of justice (at p. 55):

(1) proper training of the legal profession; (2) giving the bar greater influence in the selection of judges so as to insure expert qualifications in those who are to perform an expert's function; (3) unification of the judicial system and more effective and responsible control of judicial and administrative business; (4) *giving power to the courts to make rules of procedure* and thus giving the courts power to do what we require of them; (5) improvement of legislative law-making both in substance and in technique; and (6) thorough study of the new problems which an industrial and urban society has raised and of the means of meeting them with the jural materials at hand. (Emphasis supplied.)

This continuing vitality and emphasis on change and improvement speaks well for our legal system. It demonstrates that the law is struggling with a surprising degree of success to meet the challenges it faces. It also reinforces my view that the processes of change—such as rule-making by the courts—warrant careful analysis and study.

J. B. W.

January, 1977

REFORM OF COURT
RULE-MAKING PROCEDURES

I. Introduction

1:A. Definition of Rule-Making

The subject of this study is the curious phenomenon of court control of court practice and related matters through court-promulgated rules.[1] Although "rule-making" is sometimes used to refer to significant reformulation of decisional law, it is not used in that sense in this discussion.[2] Particularly at the federal level, the process of adopting rules for federal courts has worked fairly well for the past forty years. Rules of evidence and rules for civil, criminal, bankruptcy, and admiralty cases and appeals have been adopted and are generally acknowledged to be sound. Some disturbing issues have, however, arisen, and substantial changes should now be considered. I have placed primary emphasis on the national court system, but considerable attention is given to the states' experience because here, as elsewhere, they are effective laboratories for testing different approaches.[3]

Rule-making by courts is being exercised increasingly at national, state, and local levels. The process presents substantial advantages and serious dangers. Procedures used in exercising the power vary considerably. This is, it seems to me, an appropriate time to take stock of where we have gone and where we ought to go in the future.

Court rules have much the form and effect of legislative enactments. Until repealed or modified they control all litigation encompassed within their ambit. Like legislative enactments, they are subject to interpretation and to

3

a declaration of invalidity when they are in conflict with legislation or constitutions.

In most instances the legislature has power to amend or reject rules adopted by a court. The Federal Rules of Civil and Criminal Procedure and the Federal Rules of Evidence are typical of this subjugation of court rule-making to legislative control. New Jersey's highest court was almost unique in claiming that its power to adopt rules is not subject to legislative control; but, as is indicated below, that court has been forced to compromise this position.[4] In other instances the rules are part of an amalgam of statutory provisions adopted by the legislature and rules adopted by a court or judicial body. This is the situation in New York where the New York Civil Practice Law and Rules includes provisions adopted and modified by the legislature and those adopted by the New York State Judicial Conference, a body made up of judges, subject to legislative veto or change.[5]

Each individual court also generally has power to adopt rules affecting its own practice. At the local level there are court rules adopted by each of the federal district courts[6] and by each one of the circuit courts of appeals.[7] State courts have similar local rules.[8]

I:B. Rule-Making as Legislation

Rule-making by federal courts represents a reversal of usual adjudicative patterns. In most instances a court acts in controversies based upon particular facts on a case-by-case basis, leaving subsequent decisions to synthesize general substantive and procedural rules. At the level of national federal rule-making, the Supreme Court lays down general standards applicable to all future cases without the aid of individual fact situations and argument. The Court does not have before it interested parties with a motive for presenting the case fully, as it does in litigation meeting constitutional justiciability requirements.[9] In rule-making the Court makes legislative pronouncements reviewed by Congress—a departure from the usual instance where congressional legislation is measured and interpreted by the courts in the light of constitutional and other requirements. In normal adjudications the Court's power is based upon the Constitution, although that power is limited and proscribed by jurisdiction, venue, and other provisions enacted by Congress. In rule-making the Court's power is granted by Congress under specific limitations; having accepted that grant for many years it is doubtful whether the Court could claim inherent power were general rule-making power circumscribed. Usually a court is concerned with due process and the opportunity for those concerned to be heard publicly, whereas in rule-making a court generally acts *in camera* without providing an opportunity for argument.

Where the courts utilize a litigation to pronounce broad general principles and detailed regulations, such as the *Miranda* rules[10] designed to control police interrogations in a quasi-legislative manner, the courts are subject to the restrictions imposed by judicial tradition.[11] Such cases involve the concreteness of a litigated matter with specific facts presenting the issue and with opposing counsel strenuously arguing different points of view. Public argument is normally afforded and briefs by the parties and by amici may be submitted. The court is obligated to justify its decision by a reasoned opinion.[12] Moreover, the possibility exists of relatively easy modification through future interpretations and legislation, though change becomes awkward when the decision is justified by constitutional imperatives.[13]

In the case of legislation, there are equivalent protections to a reasoned determination acceptable to the public. The legislation must be publicly introduced. There is normally the requirement of a number of readings with consideration by committees and an opportunity of the public to make its views heard,[14] through representatives of pressure groups. At hearings and sessions marking up bills, various hypothetical and actual situations and precedents will be tested against the draft to minimize dangers due to careless articulation of the legislative standard. The representatives in the legislative body will normally bring to bear different backgrounds and the interests of the particular geographical and other groups that they represent. Each legislator knows that he or she may be compelled to justify a vote at an election.[15] There is, too, the opportunity to place pressure on the executive, before the bill is approved. These are all very real protections in a democratic system. Even though court rules rarely involve matters that excite public controversy, the right of the public to be heard on legislation is too important to be needlessly attenuated.

The court rule-making process does not necessarily allow the same kind of protections for the public. Most of the discussion and decision-making takes place privately. The first time the public is aware of the rule may be upon its publication after adoption. This is particularly true of local rules. Important matters involving size of juries, sentencing policy in connection with certain crimes, policy with respect to class actions, opportunity of the press to publicize cases, admission to the bar, and the like, are decided privately by a group of judges. Their decision is then announced as a local rule without any opportunity for the public to debate what has been done or to appear at any announced meeting to oppose the rule. Sometimes, as in the case of guidelines issued by higher courts, there is no publication and the public is not made aware of criteria that will control judges' decisions.

Generally, the United States Supreme Court has adopted rules with considerable protection to the public. The rules are published in advance by the advisory committee considering them; opportunity is then given to the public to comment to the advisory committee in writing; the advisory committee publishes revised drafts; the Standing Committee on Federal Rules of Practice and Procedure of the United States Judicial Conference reviews the proposals and makes changes; the United States Judicial Conference forwards them to the Supreme Court; that Court then adopts, modifies, or rejects; and Congress has an opportunity to pass upon them.

Within the last few years Congress has taken a more vigorous interest in national rules. It has held hearings and made major modifications in the Federal Rules of Evidence and recent amendments to the Federal Rules of Criminal Procedure.

Even at the national level, however, the deliberations of the advisory committee, which makes the basic deci-

sions, are private. It holds no public hearings. It does
receive written communications, but its membership and
method of organization may make it particularly suscep-
tible to the views of the courts, groups represented by its
members, and governmental bodies. Appointment of
members by the Chief Justice gives him a great deal of
direct and indirect influence on its decisions.

I:C. Disenchantment with Current
Rule-Making Process

My personal experience as well as studies have gradu-
ally led me to the view that additional protections need
to be built into rule-making. My interest in the matter of
rule-making began to sharpen many years ago when I
first taught at the Law School of Columbia University.
The course was largely organized around the Federal
Rules of Civil Procedure.[16] In a number of instances I
wondered whether there had been sufficient study and
public debate before adoption.[17] One matter of some
concern was the ability of any court to remain impartial
in its consideration of a rule when an attack was made
upon the rule's wisdom or constitutionality, since the
same body that promulgated the rule was passing upon
it.

When I was appointed reporter to the Advisory Committee on Practice and Procedure of a commission (and
later a legislative committee) seeking to reform New
York procedure, the enormous improvement in practice
resulting from the federal rules and their great prestige
led me to propose placing rule-making power in the New
York Court of Appeals, according to the federal

model.[18] For a variety of political and other reasons the New York legislature rejected this plan. After a series of compromises it adopted the New York Civil Practice Law and Rules, leaving some matters for rule-making by the State Judicial Conference of Judges. By the time of this compromise my support for uncontrolled court rule-making, as called for by Wigmore and Chief Judge Vanderbilt of New Jersey, had cooled considerably. The New York compromise, therefore, seemed to me a workable experiment, and it had the added glamour of being the best we could get.[19] Since the New York Judicial Conference relies upon a distinguished advisory group of lawyers and law professors with supporting studies undertaken at the law schools, the compromise provides a satisfactory basis for new rules and for new legislation dealing with procedure.

Upon being appointed to the Advisory Committee on the Federal Rules of Evidence by Chief Justice Warren, I again became enmeshed in the drafting of rules. This was a most impressive venture. The other members of the committee were judges, law professors, and practicing lawyers of talent, experience, and dedication. The chairman, Albert E. Jenner, was a truly outstanding leader in law reform, and the reporter, Edward W. Cleary, had had experience in the drafting of procedural rules in Illinois and had an impressive background in evidence law. During the more than a half dozen years that I worked with this committee I enjoyed one of the greatest educational experiences it is possible to have in the law.[20]

Nevertheless, there were disquieting aspects to the work.[21] For one thing, there was no equivalent to the oral presentations from the public during deliberations and to the open debate among members that took place when Congress ultimately considered the matter. The advisory committee did, of course, have extensive written submissions from bar association committees and individuals all over the country. The criticism by Judge Friendly that the profession was not aware of what the committee was doing, to the extent that it was justified, was not due to any lack of effort on the part of the advisory committee. Its drafts were published widely, and its members spoke at many meetings of lawyers. Even after the final draft was completed and it was returned by the Supreme Court for further work, additional comments were received by the public, and additional published drafts were made available. The fact is, however, that it is difficult to get lawyers interested in the process until after the rules are effective and it is necessary to learn them.

Our proposed rules on privileges would have had an impact on a variety of groups such as doctors and newsmen, and yet there was only one occasion when outsiders addressed the group. It was a rather unsatisfactory session; two doctors appeared and there was a sense of annoyance at this interjection of outside persons into the committee's deliberations.

Some criticism was also made that the advisory committee had no representatives of some of the younger groups in the law profession, such as those representing poverty agencies. Where our drafts would have made it easier or more difficult to convict those accused of crime, conservative elements of Congress, represented by Senator McClellan, and the Department of Justice probably had an impact greater than that of other individuals and organizations, particularly during the later stages of our work, since there was no opportunity for counter-forces to publicly debate the issues.[22]

There were some, therefore, who were pleased to see Congress take an interest in the matter, conduct full hearings, and reach some decisions different from the Supreme Court's. Whether the rules as promulgated by the Supreme Court were on balance improved by Congress is debatable. In any event, there had been a full ventilation of the issues through normal legislative procedures. Although the decisions of Congress will probably not have a significant impact on litigation, except, perhaps, in the area of privileges, they did ensure that everyone who wanted to be was heard by those charged with adoption.

Similarly, in connection with the 1975 revisions of the Rules of Criminal Procedure, Congress took an active role, holding public hearings and making extensive revisions. Despite the conclusion of Congressman William L. Hungate, the able chairman of the House Judiciary Sub-Committee, which held the hearings, that the rules as adopted by Congress were not improved over the rules promulgated by the Court,[23] the rules, as ultimately amended, did have an aura of legitimacy that they theretofore might have lacked.

As a United States district judge, I have been increasingly disturbed by the relatively unchecked power of courts, including my own, to adopt local rules.[24] Some of them have very important substantive and procedural impacts. They are generally promulgated without any warning or public debate.

11

*I:D. Advantages of Rule-Making in
Meeting Growing Pressures on Courts*

Despite these problems, rule-making has substantial advantages. In understanding them it is useful to glance back historically and to consider the issue in a broader context than today's events. It is desirable in this connection to touch lightly on the concept of advisory opinions as compared to the common law case-by-case method. We should also consider briefly the problem of separation of powers and the necessity in many instances of bridging that separation by practical expedients.

We must also bear in mind the enormous pressure on American courts both to adjudicate large numbers of individual cases and to intervene in major social, economic, technical, and political matters. The result has been both a large increase in the judicial system, with all the administrative and other problems attendant on a change in scale, and constant emphasis on the need for more "efficiency."

Increased use of the rule-making power is but one manifestation of growing court intervention in this country. The reasons for this increased reliance on courts are complex, and I do not pretend to understand the matter fully. But, among them are the following: First, large institutions, including government, have assumed greater control over society. When I was younger we called this syndrome the managerial revolution. In part, we were seeing a reaction to laissez-faire economic policy that had been predominant in this country for some generations. There has been, for a half century, a strong belief—now perhaps waning—that social science and political tools

12

can positively control society by means analogous to the methods used to exercise scientific and technological control over nature. Concurrently, we have drifted away from reliance on independent small social forces to balance each other.

Second, there is growing recognition that most individuals are unable to successfully confront big government or big business except in conjunction with equalizing formal organizations such as unions and conservation groups. Informal ad hoc organizations, such as in class actions, or substantial court or legislative intervention serve an equivalent function.

Third, there has been by now a habituation to the placing of massive control burdens on the courts, requiring exercise of powers on a grand scale. The power to declare legislation unconstitutional in *Marbury*[25] has been increasingly utilized against the states. The fourteenth amendment and the control over various state legislative activities has increased the power of the courts. So, too, has the growth of federal legislation, as for example, in the welfare area, which requires the courts to intervene frequently in connection with challenges to the constitutionality and legality of a variety of state programs.[26] In some areas, as in the antitrust field, where the power was imposed by Congress, the courts have had to exercise control over huge businesses.

Fourth, there has been, we are all aware, a growing tempo of social and technological change. In many instances the legislature has failed to act to meet new situations because of a balance of forces preventing adoption of an affirmative program. As a result, in fields such as race and sex discrimination, welfare, jail reorganization, abortion, reapportionment, and fair trial for the accused, the courts have stepped in to make necessary adjustments in the law.

Fifth, there is an expectation of the public that the government will act to meet problems insoluble by individuals. Failure of the legislature to meet that hope has caused the public to look increasingly to the courts.

Sixth, federal courts have had fairly good public relations. The Supreme Court and other federal courts have been relatively free of scandal. There is, perhaps, too, the black robe syndrome of people looking for a father figure during troubled times.

Rules, like legislation, permit a whole multitude of possible procedural and related issues to be decided at once, with a possible saving of judicial energy in individual cases. At the least, well-drafted rules should save judges and lawyers expensive case-law research time. A good set of rules should—in theory—also reduce appeals and reversals on nonsubstantive points. By providing more efficient court procedures, they allow courts and lawyers to accomplish more with the same expenditure of energy, enabling us to better meet the pressures of more, and more complex, litigation.

The present situation is to be contrasted with that when the republic was in its infancy. The courts were accustomed to handling individual cases, which were in the main brought by one real person against another for relatively modest relief. The theory was that the rules of law—procedure as well as substance—developed by accretion through decision in individual cases, permitting from time to time a synthesis of prior decisions and a modest generalization that would represent a step forward. Dicta was, of course, not unknown, and the courts were clearly aware of the prospective nature of their rulings in individual cases and of the impact of stare decisis on the law. The concept of separation of powers was, however, adhered to. The courts, at the federal level at least, refused to render advisory opinions.[27]

This restrictive model of the courts' role began to break down early in this century. Antitrust cases requiring the courts to make national economic policy were one of the harbingers of a different approach. So, too, was the Brandeis brief recognizing explicitly that underlying substantive social policy was being developed by the courts. Broad cases involving attacks on state legislative schemes as in the public welfare disputes of the twenties and thirties were accepted. Wide-ranging judicial intervention has been prompted in large part by the growth of legislative patterns that control great segments of society. Judicial intervention has also been encouraged by the tendency of Congress to modify substantive rights in ways that require the courts to resolve individual disputes involving large groups of persons and entities.[28] For example, statutory interpretations of Title VII legislation[29] covering discrimination in employment has involved the courts in intricate opinions connected with methods of testing and selecting of municipal and private employees. Fortunately, courts have been assisted by rules of the Equal Employment Opportunity Commission, which they have adopted on a wholesale basis.[30]

Heavy pressure from expanding concepts of due process, "individualized determination" as opposed to "categorical treatment,"[31] has increased the burdens of litigation.[32] Glimmers of a tendency to require less than

15

full-fledged evidentiary trials by shaping procedural due process rules to "the risk of error inherent in the truth-finding process"[33] in specific classes of cases, has promised a decrease in the growth rate of administrative hearings, but not yet in judicial trials. The force of our country's original theme of individual liberty and personal rights recently reinforced by the specter of threatening modern totalitarians has not abated; "individual decision-making"[34] on a huge scale provides a continuing challenge to our judicial system.

Faced with mounting caseloads, courts have reached out for ways to handle disputes on a wholesale rather than a retail basis wherever there was not too wrenching a disruption of prior concepts of the limitations on their roles. Modern court rules reflect these changes. Much of the environmental, consumer, and securities litigation has been made possible by an expanded class action rule, for example.[35] Free intervention rules and more flexible procedures generally have broadened the scope of litigation. Transfer and consolidation rules and statutes for pretrials and trials in multidistrict litigation have made national litigation easier.[36] Res judicata has been expanded so that disputes among many parties can be disposed of in one case.[37] Standing requirements have been reduced.[38] Mootness claims have been ignored[39] and the impact of ripeness reduced.[40] Prospective overruling has reduced the burden of retroactivity, allowing quantum jumps in substantive and procedural rights.[41] Federal courts have asked state courts for advisory opinions[42] and states have granted them more frequently.[43] Warnings of changes to come, as in pre-*Mapp v. Ohio*[44] cases, have reduced inhibitions on new changes. There has been a tendency to write opinions like "legislative codes."[45]

We have seen the growth of organizations such as the NAACP Legal Defense Fund, the American Civil Liberties Union, and the Sierra Club. They are capable of orchestrating the development of an entire area of the law, such as desegregation of schools, capital punishment, abortion, environment, and the like.[46]

The rule-making power that we are particularly concerned with is a development in tune with these others. It extends the reach of judicial power by making courts more efficient and by permitting a single decision—whether in a case or by rule—to have a wider impact.

I:E. Rule-Making Process as an Exercise in Pragmatism

Given these developments, we must return to the problem of how the rule-making power is to be exercised. We tend to think, based on recent experience, that the courts have been more progressive with respect to rules of procedure, court reform, and the like compared to legislatures,[47] but this has not always been the case. It should be recalled that in England procedural reform of the old common law system was based on legislative initiative following attacks on the courts led by reformers like Jeremy Bentham. As Sunderland noted, "[T]he continuous initiative which theory seems to ascribe to the judges in making the rules will appear . . . to be largely non-existent."[48]

In this country the great procedural reforms of the nineteenth century were sparked by adoption of the

17

Field Code by the New York legislature, not by the courts. Much of the subsequent reform in New York and other states has been by the legislature. More recently, in England, reform of the rules of evidence was effected not by court-adopted rules or by changes in practice on a case-by-case basis, but rather by legislative revamping, including abolition of the hearsay rule in civil cases. There are now pending in England similar changes in criminal procedure, but they will be adopted, if they are adopted at all, by the legislature.

There is an enormous diversity in rule-making among the states.[49] This variation suggests that the details of the rule-making process, and particularly the degree of legislative and court control, represent a practical rather than a theoretical division of powers. So long as legislatures and courts treat each other's role with a degree of respect, almost any of the many systems at work in this country can provide effective court procedures.[50] Recommendations of the American Bar Association Commission on Standards of Judicial Administration suggest placing primary authority in the court system—not necessarily in a specific court—with ultimate supervisory power in the legislature.

Section 1.31 Rule-Making Authority.

A court system should have authority to prescribe rules of procedure, civil and criminal. The authority should extend to all proceedings in all courts in the system and should include all aspects of procedure, including rules of evidence. The authority should be exercised through a procedure that involves opportunity on the part of the public and the bar to suggest, review and make recommendations concerning proposed rules. The rule-making body should have staff assistance

18

for research and drafting. The procedure should also involve either:

(a) A requirement that proposed rules of procedure be laid before the legislature for a specified time before becoming legally effective and be subject to disapproval by a majority vote of each house of the legislature; or

(b) Provision for participation on the part of legislators and members of the bar to serve as additional members of the rule-making body or in an advisory capacity to it.[51]

In a number of states, including the two most populous ones, rules are not adopted by the highest court, but by another body. In California it is the Judicial Council consisting of representatives of the various courts.[52] In New York it is the Judicial Conference with representatives of the various courts.[53] As Parness and Korbakes point out, "in the absence of complete uniformity among all the state judicial systems, we believe that no single model could be devised which would be appropriate for all jurisdictions."[54]

The truth is that the initiative for a change in the field of procedure must come from a variety of sources—the bar, law schools, the courts, the legislature, and the public at large. What is important is that the initiative be freely available through open channels so that there is no blockage of necessary changes, while at the same time there is ample opportunity for evaluation of the fresh ideas that may come from any one of these sources. "The true test of the efficiency of any plan will be found in its capacity to maintain over the years a flexible system of procedure closely adjusted to the changing needs of society."[55]

A rule-making balance that recognizes initiative from the courts, permits legislative changes, and allows the bench, bar, and the public to actively participate in the rule-making process, constitutes a useful and practical balance. Relatively slight changes are needed, I believe, to open up the rule-making function to more public scrutiny and control, particularly at the local level. At the national level, and to some extent at the intermediate appellate level, it is necessary to ensure that positions taken during the rule-making process do not hinder a court, when hearing individual cases, from exercising an unbiased judgment. The following discussion indicates the reasons for these conclusions about where the rule-making power presently should be lodged and how it should be exercised.

II. Development of National Rule-making Power

Procedures tend to be considered timeless by those who know no other system. Present methods of writing national rules, since they have been essentially the same for the past forty years, will be assumed by many to be writ in stone. It is essential, if we are to consider change with unhooded eyes, to glance back over our history as a predicate for understanding that options are open to us. Much of the section that follows is designed to demonstrate that there are no constitutional, theoretical, or historical barriers to change.

The extent and nature of rule-making power of federal courts is inextricably intertwined with attitudes about the function of courts in relation to other branches of government and about the limits of judicial independence. The rule-making power has, nevertheless, evolved through pragmatic choices and by largely ignoring the dilemmas posed by the theoretical underpinnings of our judicial system.

On the one hand, rule-making seems violative of the federal courts' self-imposed proscription against advisory opinions. In this view, rule-making belongs in the province of the legislature. On the other hand, courts are generally in a better position than the legislative branch to determine their procedural and evidentiary needs. Rule-making, in this view, is a crucial facet of an independent judiciary; to deprive the judiciary or rule-making authority is to mar its vital independence and impair its role as a guardian of due process.

21

Great Britain has a judiciary less independent than the United States. Nevertheless, an examintion of the development of its rule-making power provides a useful comparative model and suggests some origins of American attitudes.[56]

II:A. English Experience

English courts were one of the means used to expand the King's power against the nobility's. As provider of a scheme of justice and ultimate source of legal appeal, the King acquired additional prestige and authority. Thus from the outset there was an identification of the legal system with the crown.[57] The origin of the writ of certiorari, for example, was in the King's prerogative to review the records of his courts.[58]

Certain English courts were particularly close to the Crown. The members of the Privy Council, on the civil side, and of the Star Chamber, in criminal matters (in the period before the English revolution), maintained extensive contact with the Crown and its ministers. These two organs retained substantial powers despite the creation of the common-law courts of King's Bench, Common Bench and Exchequer, and of the equity chancery courts.

Despite the identification of the courts with the King, the common law and equity courts early developed a substantial measure of independence from the executive branch. England was developing what Montesquieu termed the spirit of the laws, that is, an environment in which independent of the laws made by men, a network of principles constantly operates to determine the nature of institutions and the legislation and laws they produce.[59] The Crown's judicial powers were victims of the process and over time were whittled away and institutionalized. For example, Coke ruled in 1607 that King James I could not, in his own person, judge any case.[60] In addition, the routine of the common law itself, where law was court-made, vested great authority and powers in the judiciary.

In the seventeenth century there were even suggestions that courts hold a power of judicial review over legislative enactments. It was Lord Bolingbroke's thesis that acts of the government must conform to the requirements of a constitution, which he defined as "that Assemblages of Laws, Institutions and Customs, derived from certain fix'd Principles of Reason, directed to certain fix'd Objects of public Good, that compose the general System, according to which the Community had agreed to be govern'd."[61] He concluded that "A Parliament cannot annul the Constitution."[62] Lord Coke's report of *Bonham's Case*,[63] contained the celebrated and controversial declaration:

And it appears in our books, that in many cases, the common law will control acts of Parliament, and sometimes adjudge them to be utterly void: for when an act of Parliament is against common right and reason, or repugnant, or impossible to be performed, the common law will controul it and adjudge such act to be void. . . .[64]

However the statement in *Bonham's Case* remained a minority view, primarily seized upon by rebellious Amer-

ican colonists. Blackstone summarized the majority attitude: "[T]o set the judicial power above that of legislature . . . would be subversive of all government."[65]

Nonetheless, prior to the American Revolution,
England was increasingly progressing toward an independent judiciary. As part of that development, English
courts garnered powers to make rules governing court
procedures. Through judicial interpretation courts controlled writs and pleadings.[66] "Before the nineteenth
century each court regulated its own internal procedure
with very little intervention by Parliament."[67]

By the nineteenth century, court control over procedure was extensive and civil procedural rules had
become notoriously complex and artificial. But the judiciary was so conservative that judiciary-directed reform
was impossible. English judges almost universally shared a
natural law view that law was mechanical and static, and
that once evolved it was a permanent and unalterable
embodiment of natural reality. In addition, the Dicken-
sian chaos of nineteenth-century English procedure was
highly remunerative to established members of the bar
and bench, which further militated against reform from
within. Moreover, the tradition of case-by-case adjudication made it difficult to radically restructure highly
sophisticated and intertwined procedures. A shift in any
particular area might have implications in other areas and
would, in any event, change the practical balance between plaintiffs or defendants. For example, providing a
new or more effective procedural remedy for lessors
against lessees would obviously have an important impact
on substantive rights.

Reform fell to Parliament. Led in part by Jeremy Bentham, procedural reforms were enacted in a series of provisions between 1825 and 1875, culminating in the Judicature Acts of 1873 to 1875.[68] What evolved was a cooperative scheme for rule-making with legislative control over the overall procedural design and with authority over details left to the courts. The Civil Procedure Act of 1833, for example, placed power in the courts to formulate procedural rules, which led to the Hilary Rules of 1834.[69] Section 17 of the Judicature Act of 1875 authorized the judges of the Supreme Court to make rules governing procedure, and together with subsequent acts, vested this power in a committee of judges.[70] Although this system did result in some major redrafting of procedure, lack of outside professional advice and the burdens of other duties led to complaints about inadequate drafting by the judges, inconvenience, and need for recodification.[71]

The British legal system presently contains three rule-making bodies. The rule-making function for the Supreme Court is now vested in a Supreme Court Rule Committee created in 1925.[72] A County Court Rules Committee was established in 1959[73] and a Matrimonial Causes Rules Committee in 1973.[74] The statutory powers of these committees are far-reaching.[75] Master Jacob, Senior Master of the Queen's Bench Division, has noted that, "almost the entire process of civil litigation in the Supreme Court is regulated and prescribed by rules of Court made by the Rule Committee."[76] The statutory responsibilities of the other committees are comparable within their respective jurisdictions.[77] Moreover, in recent years, the tendency has been to extend the powers of the Rule Committee to areas previously thought to be part of substantive law.[78]

Over the years the Supreme Court Rule Committee has been responsible for the enactment of a comprehensive code of procedure. The original rules included the most workable elements of common law procedure introduced in 1852, combined with the most useful of the rules of the Court of Chancery.[79] The rules were most recently revised in 1965.[80] As a result of parliamentary, Supreme Court, and Rule Committee reforms, Britain now has a modern system of procedure that appears to provide minimal interference with substantive law in determining outcome.[81]

The County Court and Matrimonial Causes committees have also effected significant changes in the British legal system. Thus, for example, procedures established by the Matrimonial Causes Rule Committee now permit approximately one-third of all divorce petitions to be handled informally through affidavits mailed to a court registrar.[82]

Similarly, the County Court Rule Committee has established procedures permitting small claims to be arbitrated informally by a registrar. It is estimated that two-thirds of County Court small claims cases are dealt with in this manner.[83]

It is interesting to note that recent reforms in the law of evidence in England have been enacted by Parliament. Changes in the law as it affects civil cases were recommended by the Law Reform Committee appointed by the Lord Chancellor.[84] Modifications of the rules affecting criminal trials were proposed by the Criminal Law

Revision Committee appointed by the Home Secretary. The Law Revision Committee consists of judges, practitioners, and academics, and a secretary and assistant secretary who are civil servants.[85] On at least two occasions, Parliament has authorized the rule committees to make rules affecting the law of evidence. Section 5 of the Evidence Act of 1938 authorized rules permitting courts to allow specified facts to be proved by affidavit. Section 8 of the Civil Evidence Act of 1968 authorized rules modifying statutory hearsay exceptions.

The three rule committees are organizationally centered around the Lord Chancellor, as head of the judiciary. For example, Section 99(4): of the Judicature Act of 1925, enabling "Rules of Court to be made by the Lord Chancellor *together with* any four or more" of the persons therein mentioned, vests in the Lord Chancellor a right of veto, which he may exercise on grounds of policy.[86] The Lord Chancellor's approval is, likewise, required for the enactment of rules by the other committees.[87] The veto power is, however, rarely exercised since, as indicated below, all rule proposals are initially processed in the Lord Chancellor's department prior to any official action by the committees.

The rule-making body for the Superior Common Law Courts originally consisted of the judges of the superior courts, but in 1894, its membership was extended to include practicing lawyers. The Rule Committee of the Supreme Court now consists of the Lord Chancellor, the Lord Chief Justice, the Master of the Rolls, the President of the Probate Division, four other judges, two practicing barristers and two practicing solicitors.[88] The County and Matrimonial Causes committees consist of a similar

27

combination of judges and lawyers, the one significant difference being that two court registrars also sit on these committees.[89]

All appointments to the three rules committees are made by the Lord Chancellor. It has been observed that the members of the Supreme Court Rule Committee are drawn from among the preeminent judicial officers and practicing lawyers in Britain.[90] Members of the County Court Committee are closer to the grass roots of the legal process and tend to take a livelier interest in the more technical aspects of procedure.[91]

Primary responsibility for the formulation and drafting of proposed rules falls on a small legal staff within the Lord Chancellor's department, which serves as a secretariat or central organizational agency for the three committees.[92] Although the committee members occasionally make suggestions for changes in procedure, the committees' function, in the main, is to review proposals forwarded by the Lord Chancellor's department. It has been noted that the assignment of such importance to the department:

... reflects not only the central role which the Department occupies, as the office of the Lord Chancellor, in the whole field of judicial administration, but also the crucial role of the Lord Chancellor in the exercise of the powers to make rules of the Supreme Court. Because of its position, the Department had its fingers on the pulse of practice in the Courts, and because it acts as a kind of listening-post, it is extremely sensitive to the need to fashion procedural rules for the attainment of justice, while at the same time having due regard to the dictates of economy and the needs of the legal profession. Moreover, the Department is also in close touch with current legislative projects and indeed is generally consulted in advance about provisions conferring rule-making powers or necessitating the exercise of existing powers. In a real sense, therefore, the Department fulfills a much more enlarged, active and creative role than may normally be associated with a Secretary, or even a Secretariat.[93]

The Lord Chancellor's department performs two preliminary functions: (1) the reception and analysis of proposals for changes in the rules and (2) the selection and fashioning of proposals into draft rules for ultimate consideration by the appropriate committee.

The department receives proposals from a wide variety of external sources. Thus, a judge may suggest that an existing rule is unjust and should be reviewed.[94] Other sources of proposals include legal professional bodies such as the Bar Council and Law Society, individual lawyers or members of the public, and masters and comparable officials in the several divisions of the high court.[95] The greatest source of proposals are the reports of special departmental committees on procedure.[96]

Basic decisions as to proposals meriting selection, sources outside the department to be consulted, and the wording of the draft rule, are generally entrusted to the informed discretion of key staff members.[97] On occasion priorities are dictated to the department. Thus, for example, rules required by statute or proposals from the Lord Chancellor or senior judges are given prompt attention.[98] In the main, it is up to the department's experts to determine which of the existing rules are defective or which unregulated areas are in need of regulation.

Once the department decides to consider a proposal, outside sources are consulted. This process is described as follows:

The principle which appears to be followed is, to carry through a careful and thorough consultation with all interests that may be concerned with the changes proposed. Thus, the Lord Chancellor's Department will seek, as may be necessary, the advice, assistance and guidance of the presiding or senior Judge, and of the senior Master or other equivalent, of the several Divisions of the High Court, other Judges, the Bar Council, the Law Society, and anyone else who it is thought might be able to help. These consultations are carried out on a "Confidential" basis, largely by correspondence though occasionally by oral discussions, but hardly ever at meetings arranged for the purpose, save in exceptional circumstances when a Working Party will be set up for a specified purpose, for example, the revision of the rules or to deal with a particularly difficult subject such as Hearsay Evidence. Those consulted regard it as a matter of duty to give all the help they can, though they do so willingly, even eagerly.[99]

Two additional points concerning the drafting process are worth noting. First, it is not the practice of the committees to publish draft rules for general comment and debate by the legal profession as is the case of a bill laid before Parliament. Consequently, "[t]he rules are hammered out and put into shape within a comparatively narrow but highly specialised expert and interested body of consultants, and they are only finally published if and when they are approved and made by the Rule Committee."[100] Second, advisors will rely heavily on the advice of the Lord Chancellor as to the political implications of proposed rules having substantive policy consequences.[101]

When the Lord Chancellor's department has gathered a sufficient number of draft rules it will convene a meeting of the appropriate rule committee, generally with about

a month's notice.[102]   In recent years, the committees
have usually met two or three times a year.[103]   These
meetings are closed to the public. Of the three committees, only the County Court Rule Committee keeps
minutes of the proceedings.[104]   The proceedings have
been described as follows:

> At the meeting of the Rule Committee, the Lord Chancel-
> lor, or in his absence the Lord Chief Justice, presides and he
> is assisted by members of his staff, who are concerned with
> the rules under consideration. In the ensuing discussion, the
> draft rules are subjected to a close scrutiny, more especially
> from the point of view of the policy underlying them and
> their operation in practice. Frequently, members of the
> Committee raise points on the draft rules, both as to form
> and substance. Often points are raised by the Barrister and
> Solicitor members affecting their respective branches of the
> profession. So far as possible, any doubts raised or amend-
> ments suggested are dealt with on the spot, or if this is not
> possible, they are left to be dealt with by the Lord Chancel-
> lor's Department. At the conclusion of the meeting, the
> members of the Rule Committee sign the instrument making
> the rules Rules of the Supreme Court.[105]

It has been observed that committee meetings are generally harmonious, the issue of costs being the only
recurring cause of divisiveness.[106]

After passage by the committee, a rule of court is laid
before Parliament along with an effective date, usually
determined by the Lord Chancellor. Here it will be
examined by the Scrutiny Committee of the House of
Commons. The rule becomes effective automatically,
unless a prayer against it is moved and passed by one of
the Houses of Parliament. Such legislative veto is rarely

exercised.[107]   However, the Scrutiny Committee has caused rules to be withdrawn where it was felt that the Rule Committee had exceeded its power or had allowed improper subdelegation.[108]   Subdelegation is the conferring of discretion to make individualized decisions in particular cases as distinguished from prescribing a result by means of a rule.[109]

Once effective, the rules have the force of legislation, since the committees are considered a subordinate branch of Parliament.[110]   Thereafter, they are subject to a limited judicial review as to the questions of whether they are *intra vires.* The rule-making power governs procedures only, not substance.[111]   It is apparently believed by those who have considered the issue in England that participation of judges in the work of the rule committees does not inhibit them from examining the validity of a particular rule in a particular case.[112]

As a result of these procedures, Britain by the close of the nineteenth century had evolved a balanced rule-making system. Initiative was essentially with the executive; primary authority was in the judicial branch, through the Rule Committee; but Parliament retained power to intervene. The method of reform—engaging as it does cooperative efforts of the executive, Parliament, the judges, members of the bar and of the university—turns out to be similar to that developed in this country, although there are obviously differences in detail. For one thing, the civil service under the English system is much more important than the equivalent officials here, such as members of the Administrative Office of the Courts, the Judicial Center, or Department of Justice, would be. For another, the law schools and bar in the

United States seem to have a much greater influence. There is, too, apparently a greater effort in this country to publicize proposals in advance so that suggestions can be received from the public.

The rule committees have been criticized in England for the sometimes haphazard manner in which proposals are considered and for insufficient representation of the bar and the public. But close observers feel that the present system functions efficiently and is acutely responsive to need for reform as it arises.

Master Jacob concludes:

> The machinery of rule-making . . . , although it may appear to be slow and cumbersome, nevertheless contributes in a special and crucial way both to the stability and flexibility of English procedural law. It enables the Rules of Court to be made, tested in practice, and changed from time to time as may be necessary without engaging the time or attention of Parliament, and it enables those most directly concerned with the administration of justice to devise and provide fresh procedural devices to be employed and thus to meet the changing needs of society.[113]

As in this country, pragmatism is the touchstone for making rules governing court practice and procedure. As Samuel Rosenbaum pointed out in his somewhat outdated, but still admirable, summary of the history of rule-making in England:

> It appears, therefore, that no one of the three branches of our Government is, by the theory of the Constitution or the character of the duty, so peculiarly fitted for this work that the other two must be excluded from consideration. In such a position, the guiding principle becomes one of expediency.[114]

II:B. Evolution of an Independent Federal Judiciary

The evolution of rule-making power in our country is intertwined with the relation of courts to other branches of government. The extent of judicial independence has a crucial bearing on the courts' role in rule-making.

II:B:1. State Courts in Colonial and Post-Revolutionary Eras

Insofar as colonial opinion focused on the separation of powers, it was concerned primarily with the division of authority between the executive and the legislative branches, rather than with the extent of judicial power of either of these branches. Prior to the Revolution colonists sought to assert colonial legislative power over the royal governors. The role of the judiciary was inevitably of secondary concern.

After the outbreak of the Revolution, all of the states, proceeding from English theory, Enlightenment thinking, and colonial experience, enacted constitutions as fundamental laws that generally reflected separation-of-powers doctrines. Some were more clear about separation of the judiciary from other branches than others. In New York, for example, draftsmen of the 1777 constitution, led by Robert Livingston, placed power to check the legislature in a Council of Revision composed of the governor, chancellor, and judges of the state Supreme Court, rather than in the courts. The council was empowered to reject "improper" legislation, and such legislation could not become effective unless two-thirds of each legislative house subsequently approved it.[115]   A number of states made provision for an independent judiciary. Delaware, Maryland, Massachusetts, New Hampshire, New York, and North Carolina enacted provisions protecting judges' tenure in office. Delaware, Massachusetts, New Hampshire, Pennsylvania, North Carolina, South Carolina, and Virginia insured judicial salaries against reduction.[116] In Virginia John Marshall pressed for a judiciary independent of executive restraints.[117]

However distinctions between the judiciary and other branches were occasionally blurred. Jefferson noted that on a number of occasions the Virginia Burgesses had decided controversies better determined by judicial action.[118] The executive branch in Pennsylvania, reflecting the dominance of the Penn family in the pre- and post-Revolutionary period in that state, usurped traditional judicial powers by committing persons to jail, setting bail, and interfering with civil litigation and habeas corpus proceedings.[119] The court's duty to render advisory opinions was a part of the Massachusetts constitution: "Each branch of the legislature as well as the governor and council shall have authority to require the opinions of the justices of the supreme judicial court, upon important questions of law, and upon solemn occasions."[120] Despite its early institutionalization, the advisory opinion has been sparingly used in Massachusetts; there have only been some 250 such opinions in 190 years. Variants of the Massachusetts provision have been adopted in New Hampshire, Maine, Rhode Island, Florida, Colorado, and South Dakota; and four states have statutes authorizing advisory opinions in certain circumstances.[121]

In summary, although the states advanced the notion of an independent judiciary beyond English developments, judicial separation remained imperfect. The courts did, nevertheless, continue to modify practice on a case-by-case basis without legislative intervention; *stare decisis* gave individual rulings substantial impact. Courts and the bar were actively altering practice and procedure by interstitial changes to meet the needs of a new society.[122]

II:B:2. The Constitutional Period

II:B:2:a. Debates at the Philadelphia Convention

The Articles of Confederation made no provision for a federal court system; enforcement of federal law was left to the states. The Constitution, of course, changed this situation.

The concept of separation of powers was "axiomatic in contemporary political thinking," and almost universally shared by the framers, acquired either through Enlightenment readings or colonial experience.[123] Although this attitude governed the evolution of the articles on the legislative and executive branches, it was less clearly applied by the framers to the judiciary, largely because there were few precedents for truly separate and independent courts.

Convention consideration of a framework for the judicial branch initially focused on the "Virginia Plan." Resolution 9 of this scheme, apparently drawn up by Edmund Randolph (later the first Attorney General), George Wythe (Chancellor of Virginia), and John Blair, (a future Supreme Court Justice), proposed a system of independent federal courts, supreme and inferior, that was national in attitude. Jurisdiction

of the inferior tribunals shall be to hear and determine in the dernier resort, all piracies and felonies on the high seas, captures from an enemy; cases in which foreigners or citizens of other States applying to such jurisdictions may be interested, or which respect the collection of the National revenue; impeachments of any National officers, and questions which may involve the national peace and harmony.[124]

Opposed to this scheme was a proposal of delegates of smaller states, principally designed by William Paterson of New Jersey (later a Supreme Court Justice), which envisioned a supreme court of very limited jurisdiction and no inferior federal courts. This plan, along with a similar plan advanced by Charles Pinckney of South Carolina, reflected the ambivalent attitude of the Articles of Confederation toward the judiciary, and largely rejected the national judicial power advanced by the Virginians' plan. The Virginia Plan eventually won, although elements of Paterson's and Pinckney's plans were retained.

The Virginia Plan was not pure in its attitude toward judicial independence. Resolution 8 of the plan provided for a Council of Revision composed of the executive and members of the judiciary. Modeled on the one established by New York's Constitution of 1777, the council was granted power to review all acts of the national legislature before they became operative, including legislative vetoes of state laws. This proposition was attacked by Elbridge Gerry of Massachusetts as an improper merger of the judiciary with the executive and as unnecessary since courts would in any event possess "a sufficient check agst. encroachments on their own department by their exposition of the laws which involved a power of deciding on their Constitutionality."[125] Eventually a proposal to leave veto power in executive hands, subject to reversal by two-thirds of each branch, was substituted.

But power to check the legislative branch was not left exclusively to executive veto. At the close of the first debates on the judiciary, the delegates unanimously approved a resolution similar to one of Paterson's proposals. It stated that federal legislation would override any conflicting state laws, and as a result, the state judiciary would have to enforce this supremacy. It provided in part:

that the legislative Acts of the United States made by virtue and in pursuance of the articles of Union and all Treaties made and ratified under authority of the United States shall be the supreme law of the respective States as far as those acts or Treaties shall relate to the said States, or their Citizens and Inhabitants—and that the Judiciaries of the several States shall be bound thereby in their decisions any thing in the respective laws of the individual States to the contrary notwithstanding.[126]

Judicial control over state enactments in conflict with federal laws provided a conceptual springboard to judicial control over congressional enactments conflicting with the Constitution.

This final leap was in large part made in the final weeks of the convention during the debate over the supremacy clause. The draft of the convention's Committee of Detail stated that "the jurisdiction of the Supreme Court shall extend to all cases arising under the laws passed by the legislature of the United States." Professor Goebel summarizes what happened next:

[William Samuel] Johnson [delegate from Connecticut] moved the insertion of "this Constitution and the," so that the phrase read "the jurisdiction of the Supreme Court shall extend to all cases under this Constitution and the laws passed by the legislature. . . ." The effect of this was to place beyond question the role of the Supreme Court as arbiter of the Constitution. . . . The vote on the motion was unanimous.

No less significant was the passage of Rutledge's motion to delete from the clause under discussion the words "passed by the legislature," already eliminated in the supreme law provision. Even if the laymen present did not realize it, to a lawyer the words as they now read—"the laws of the United States" —opened the door to a substantial accretion of magisterial authority by the removal of the limitation to enactments. Almost as an afterthought, for it was to make the section further conform to the Committee's supremacy clause, cases arising under treaties were inserted. Finally the two pugnacious nationalists, Madison and Morris, capped the repair of the section by moving the substitution of the words the "judicial power" in place of the words the "jurisdiction of the Supreme Court." To speak of jurisdiction in terms of national power and not of a court was a noteworthy extension of the base of judicial authority.[127]

This final version of the section sowed the seeds of the notion of judicial review, leaving them ripening for Marshall's subsequent reaping in *Marbury v. Madison*.[128] In all, seventeen of the fifty-five delegates at the convention stated that federal courts were empowered to pass on the constitutionality of Congressional acts. As Corwin notes,

> True these are only seventeen names out of a possible fifty-five, but let it be considered whose names they are. They designate fully three-fourths of the leaders of the Convention, four of the five members of the Committee of Detail which drafted the Constitution, and four of the five members of the Committees of Style which gave the Constitution final form. The entries under these names in the Index to Farrand's Records occupy fully thirty columns, as compared with fewer than half as many columns under the names of the remaining members. We have in this list, in other words, the names of men who expressed themselves on the subject of judicial review because they also expressed themselves on all other subjects before the Convention. They were the leaders of that body and its articulate members.[129]

The Philadelphia convention had conceived a judiciary of unprecedented power and independence. It was to include a system of inferior courts as well as a Supreme Court, it was explicitly empowered to review actions of the state courts, and it was implicitly empowered to review the constitutionality of acts of Congress. Additional provisions protecting judges' salaries and tenure and establishing the dimensions of federal jurisdiction further emphasized the judiciary's independence and authority.

II:B:2:b. The Federalist Papers

The seven *Federalist Papers* dealing with the judiciary, numbers 75 to 82, all written by Hamilton, further emphasize the theme of judicial independence and authority. *Federalist* number 78 forms the conceptual heart of Hamilton's attitude toward the judiciary. He first cites Montesquieu for the proposition that "there is no liberty, if the power of judging be not separated from the legislative and executive powers."[130] Although an individual may on occasion be oppressed by the courts, essentially the courts exist to preserve individual liberties, and they will perform this function "so long as the judiciary remains truly distinct from both the legislature and executive."[131] He declares:

that as liberty can have nothing to fear from the judiciary alone, but would have every thing to fear from its union with either of the other departments; that, as all the effects of such a union must ensue from a dependence of the former on the latter, notwithstanding a nominal and apparent separation; that as, from the natural feebleness of the judiciary, it is in continual jeopardy of being overpowered, awed or influenced by its co-ordinate branches; that, as nothing can contribute so much to its firmness and independence as *permanency in office,* this quality may therefore be justly regarded as an indispensable ingredient in its constitution; and in a great measure, as the *citadel* of the public justice and public security.[132]

Hamilton's conclusion is that, "The complete independence of the courts of justice is peculiarly essential in a limited constitution."[133]

Judicial independence is particularly essential since, Hamilton argued, federal courts hold the power of judicial review. The Constitution was a limited one, that is, the extent of legislative intrusion on the states and individuals was specifically limited by it.

Limitations of this kind can be preserved in practice no other way than through the medium of the courts of justice; whose duty it must be to declare all acts contrary to the manifest tenor of the constitution void. Without this, all the reservations of particular rights or privileges would amount to nothing.[134]

Arguing for judicial review of legislation's constitutionality, he denied that it made the courts more powerful than the legislature. Judicial review

only supposes that the power of the people is superior to both [judicial and legislative power]; and that where the will of the legislature declared in its statutes, stands in opposition to that of the people declared in the constitution, the judges ought to be governed by the latter rather than the former. They ought to regulate their decisions by the fundamental laws, rather than by those which are not fundamental.[135]

Because of the crucial role performed by the courts, Hamilton argued that their separation and independence must be carefully protected.

II:B:2:c. State Ratification Debates

State debates over the adoption of the Federal Constitution centered on antifederalist fears of centralized executive and legislative powers to the detriment of the powers of states and the rights of individuals; they dealt only infrequently with the judicial branch. Professor Main concluded that, "[M]ost Antifederalists were satisfied with all or with the greater part of the judiciary article; the need for a national court system was nowhere challenged and most of its powers were accepted without

question."[136]   In connection with the state debates on
the judiciary article and the importance of the concept
of separation of powers, Professor Goebel agreed, noting
that

> The pro-Constitution men enjoyed one great advantage. No
> one seriously challenged the basic validity of the tripartite
> division of powers. This had become a fundamental of the
> American political credo, thanks to the almost apocalyptic
> quality attributed to Montesquieu's *Esprit des Lois.* Conse-
> quently, even the most ardent advocates of the *status quo*
> conceded grudgingly or *sub silentio* the propriety of making
> better provision for the exercise of judicial power in matters
> of national concern than the very limited concessions in the
> Articles of Confederation.[137]

The ratification debates in Virginia were the most
thoughtful. The Virginia antifederalists were led by
Patrick Henry and George Mason, who had opposed the
Constitution as a delegate at the Philadelphia convention.
Mason had drafted the Virginia Declaration of Rights,
which greatly influenced the Declaration of Independence and the Bill of Rights, and had served, with George
Wythe, Virginia's leading Enlightenment political philoso-
pher in the pre- and post-Revolutionary period.[138]
Mason attacked article III at the ratification convention,
insisting that it would place the states and their courts in
an entirely subservient role to the federal judiciary.[139]
Madison, leading the federalists at the convention, defended on the ground that the federal jurisdiction envisioned in article III was limited and necessary to prevent
controversies affecting the nation as a whole from being
left to partial local forums.[140]   Marshall, another federal-

ist delegate, even argued that antifederalists should welcome a powerful federal judiciary as a check on other federal officials.

If they were to make a law not warranted by any of the powers enumerated, it would be considered by the judges as an infringement of the Constitution which they are to guard. They would not consider such a law as coming under their jurisdiction. They would declare it void.[141]

Marshall's enunciation of a theory of judicial review was the conceptual high-water mark of the state ratification debates over the judiciary article, and prefigured his strong assertion of independent judicial power as Chief Justice.[142]

The degree to which the independence and authority of the federal judiciary was taken for granted would seem to indicate that there would be minimal opposition to judicial rule-making. But the courts themselves defined doctrines—stemming largely from their interpretation of the constitutional requirement that judicial power extend to cases and controversies—such as the advisory opinion rule, that could cast doubt on whether or not courts could make rules outside the context of a particular law suit.

II:C. Advisory Opinions

The development of the advisory opinion rule provides a useful model for exploration of judicial independence and its relation to rule-making after the adoption of the Constitution. This is the subject to which we now turn.

On July 18, 1793, Thomas Jefferson, then Secretary of State, wrote a lengthy letter to Chief Justice John Jay and the Associate Justices of the Supreme Court seeking their advice.[143]   Attached to the letter was a long list of questions. The following question was typical:

Do the treaties between the United States and France give to France or her citizens a *right,* when at war with a power with whom the United States are at peace, to fit out originally in and from the ports of the United States vessels armed for war, with or without commission?[144]

On August 8, 1793, after waiting for the Court to assemble, Jay and the Justices replied, refusing to give extrajudicial advice.[145]   The Justices placed the bar against rendering advisory opinions to other branches on the strongest conceptual ground: the constitutional requirement of separation of powers. In so doing they rejected contemporary precedent that allowed courts to render advisory opinions.[146]

There are, nevertheless, instances where federal courts have not followed the bar against advisory opinions. On April 10, 1792, the Circuit Court for the District of New York, with John Jay presiding as Circuit Justice, unanimously protested against an act of Congress[147]   providing that applications from Revolutionary War veterans for invalid pensions should be evaluated and payments fixed by judges of the circuit courts.[148]   Their protest stated that Congress could not assign to the judiciary

any duties but such as are properly judicial, and to be performed in a judicial manner. That the duties assigned to the Circuit Courts by this act are not of that description, . . . inasmuch as it subjects the decisions of these courts, made pursuant to those duties, first to the consideration and suspension of the secretary at war, and then to the revision of the legislature; whereas, by the Constitution, neither the secretary at war, nor any other executive officer, nor even the legislature are authorized to sit as a court of errors on the judicial acts or opinions of this court.[149]

Two other circuit courts initiated similar petitions, one of them declaring that the courts could not perform the pension regulation envisioned by the act:

1st. Because the business directed by this act is not of a judicial nature. It forms no part of the power vested by the constitution in the courts of the United States; the circuit court must, consequently, have proceeded *without* constitutional authority.

2d. Because, if, upon that business, the court had proceeded, its *judgments* (for its *opinions* are *judgments*) might, under the same act, have been revised and controlled by the legislature, and by an officer in the executive department. Such revision and control we have deemed radically inconsistent with the independence of that judicial power which is vested in the courts; and consequently, with that important principle which is so strictly observed by the constitution of the United States.[150]

The issue of pension rulings later came up in *Hayburn*'s case,[151] but before the Supreme Court decided the case, the issue was mooted by congressional repeal of the offending act.[152]

These extrajudicial protests are intriguing since they are plainly advisory to the executive and legislative branches, outside of a case or controversy. On the other hand, they relied upon a theory of judicial independence, and mark, in a practical sense, the first stated claim by federal courts to the power to declare congressional acts unconstitutional.

In 1790, President Washington wrote to the Justices of the Supreme Court as they were about to begin their first circuit-riding, inviting them to feel free to communicate with him from time to time concerning the judiciary system.[153]   Facing the grim and exhausting task of circuit-riding required by the Judiciary Act of 1789, Jay and a minority of the Associate Justices responded to Washington that they believed the circuit-riding requirement to be unconstitutional.[154]   There followed several other attempts by Jay to alter the circuit-riding task, none of them successful despite Washington's sympathy.[155]   The substantive issue of the constitutionality of the circuit-riding provision was raised in a case in 1801, but the Court summarily disposed of the issue on the ground that the practice was too well established by that time to be disturbed.[156]

Direct communication by the Court to the Chief Executive reflects the reality that the courts must approach Congress and the President when their assistance is needed to make the courts more effective. Requests for rule-making power by Chief Justices Taft and Hughes, annual opinions on pending legislation affecting the courts by the Judicial Conference of the United States, and requests for higher pay for federal judges by Chief Justice Burger are examples of this tradition. It is also interesting to note that, with respect to the first advisory opinion mentioned, the existence of circuit-riding for a mere quarter of a century influenced the

Court to acknowledge congressional control over court practice. In this bicentennial year we reflect back on 185 years of court exercise of rule-making powers pursuant to legislative rather than inherent authority, making it unlikely that the legislature's power can now be successfully challenged.

Another direct communication between the Court and the executive occurred in the 1820s. President Monroe, concerned about the constitutionality of his program for internal improvements, submitted a long argument supporting it to the Supreme Court. Despite the absence of any case or controversy, Justice Johnson, with the approval of the other Justices, responded that he had been

instructed to make the following Report. The Judges are deeply sensible of the mark of Confidence bestowed on them in this Instance and should be unworthy of that Confidence did they attempt to conceal their real Opinion. Indeed to conceal or disavow it would now be impossible as they are all of Opinion that the Decision on the Bank question [*McCulloch v. Maryland,* 4 Wheaton 316 (1819)] completely commits them on the Subject of internal Improvements as applied to Post-roads and Military Roads. On the other Points it is impossible to resist the lucid and conclusive Reasoning contained in the argument.[157]

In the last significant episode involving Supreme Court Justices rendering advisory opinions, Chief Justice Roger Taney wrote to the Treasury Department complaining that an 1862 tax levied on the salaries of all federal officers was invalid as applied to judges as a diminution of judges' compensation. He argued that his letter was an

48

appropriate form of protest since all judges would be disqualified if the issue arose in litigation.[158] Nonetheless, when the question later arose in connection with the federal income tax, the issue was resolved in actual litigation.[159]

Chief Justice Hughes concluded in 1928 after reviewing these early advisory opinions, that "it is safe to say that nothing of the sort could happen today."[160] In *Muskrat v. United States*,[161] the Court insisted that a congressional attempt to confer jurisdiction on the Court of Claims and, on appeal, on the Supreme Court, to determine the validity of congressional acts concerning Indians without an accompanying case or controversy was an unconstitutional invasion of the separation of powers.[162]

Since the advisory opinion doctrine made it impossible for Congress and the executive to obtain legal advice on pressing questions from the federal courts, it was forced to turn elsewhere. The advisory opinion function was absorbed by the Attorney General.[163] With the advent of extensive federal regulation of the business sector during the New Deal, advisory opinions became crucial to enable businesses to engage in reasonable planning. Thus federal regulatory agencies, despite their quasi-judicial function, regularly provide advisory opinions.[164]

During the New Deal, when, because of the delay in pressing litigation, a program would be fully operational before the Supreme Court passed upon constitutionality, there was again pressure on the Court to render advisory opinions. Senator Lewis Baxter Schwellenbach in 1937 requested the Supreme Court to amend its rules to enable the Congress on a majority vote of each house to request and receive "advisory opinions as to the constitutionality of legislation pending before, and being considered by, the Congress of the United States."[165] Senator Burton Wheeler of Montana, chairman of the Senate Judiciary Committee, inquired about the Court's attitude toward Roosevelt's court-packing plan, but Chief Justice Hughes declined to comment.[166]

It is importnat to note that the prohibition against advisory opinions emerged in the context of interaction between the judiciary and the other two branches of government, and was rationalized primarily on separation of powers grounds to protect the judiciary from intrusion by the other branches. Since judicial rule-making also involves at its heart a question of the appropriate division of roles among the three branches, it is necessary to consider whether judicial rule-making is at odds with the traditional reluctance of the courts to render advisory opinions.

The advisory opinion doctrine is not the sole obstacle. The concept of justiciability also defines judicial power, and as a result, may limit the power of courts to make rules. However, because justiciability is once again a court-defined doctrine stemming from an understanding of the requirements of the case and controversy requirement of article III, its boundaries are elusive. As Chief Justice Warren noted in *Flast v. Cohen*:[167] "The "many subtle pressures" which cause policy considerations to blend into the constitutional limitations of Article III make the justiciability doctrine one of uncertain and shifting contours."

In *United States v. Fruehauf,*[168] the court noted that often constitutional suits "are not pressed before the

Court with that clear concreteness provided when a question emerges precisely framed and necessary for decision from a clash of adversary argument exploring every aspect of a multi-faced situation embracing conflicting and demanding interests."[169]   As a result,

the Article III prohibition against advisory opinions reflects the complementary constitutional considerations expressed by the justiciability doctrine: Federal judicial power is limited to those disputes which confine federal courts to a role consistent with a system of separated powers and which are traditionally thought to be capable of resolution through the judicial process.[170]

Thus the justiciability doctrine, as well as the advisory opinion doctrine, of necessity blends policy considerations and constitutional requirements,[171] and the two are not always separable.[172]

Professors Hart and Wechsler have set forth a perceptive list of factors to consider in evaluating the need for decisions made in the face of an actual controversy:

(a) The sheer multiplication of matters to which attention must be directed, and the resulting dispersion of thought, when a legal proposition is being formulated in the abstract;

(b) The special disadvantages of dispersion of thought when a legal proposition is being formulated by a process of reasoned development of authoritative premises rather than by such a process, for example, as that by which statutes are enacted;

(c) The importance, in the judicial development of law, of a concrete set of facts as an aid to the accurate formulation of the legal issue to be decided—the weight, in other words, which should be given to the maxim, *ex facto ius oritur*;

51

(d) The importance of an adversary presentation of evidence as an aid to the accurate determination of the facts out of which the legal issue arises;

(e) The importance of an adversary presentation of argument in the formulation and decision of the legal issue;

(f) The importance of a concrete set of facts limiting the scope of the legal determination and as an aid to its accurate interpretation;

(g) The diminished scope of the play of personal convictions or preferences with respect to public policy when decision is focused upon a definite legal issue derived from a concrete set of facts;

(h) The value of having courts function as organs of the sober second thought of the community appraising action already taken, rather than as advisers at the front line of governmental action at the stage of initial decision;

(i) The importance of all the factors enumerated in maximizing the acceptability of decisions, and the importance of acceptable decisions.[173]

They go on to suggest that

the judicial function is essentially the function of . . . authoritative application to particular situations of general propositions drawn from preexisting sources—including as a necessary incident the function of determining the facts of the particular situation and of resolving uncertainties about the content of the applicable general propositions.[174]

The question emerges, then, whether judicial rule-making violates the prohibition against advisory opinions or the more fundamental definition of the judicial function embodied in the concept of justiciability.

Rule-making is only partially controlled by the advisory opinion doctrine. Like advisory opinions, rule-making occurs outside the focus of a case or controversy. In a sense rule-making raises the separation of powers issue at the heart of the ban on advisory opinions, since rule-making solely by courts would represent an infringement on legislative power to make general laws for the structure of governmental processes, including the courts. But, as the Supreme Court suggested in *Flast,* in discussing the issue of justiciability, policy considerations as well as doctrinaire constitutional theory must be taken into account.

Whereas the emergence of the separation of powers concept in the constitutional debates and the development of the doctrine of judicial review underline a growing judicial independence, the experience with the advisory opinion concept indicates that the boundaries of this independence are blurred to some extent, to accommodate practical realities.

There has never been a fully compartmentalized separation of powers. As Justice Tom Clark candidly pointed out, "The truth of it is, that there is much commingling, intermingling, and meddling among the three branches of federal government."[175] "[T]he separate powers were not intended to operate with absolute independence."[176] "[T]he framers were too sophisticated to believe that the three branches of government were absolutely separate, air-tight compartments."[177] Chief Justice Burger termed the view that the legislative and judicial branches should not talk to each other "a naive position not consistent with our constitutional system."[178] And as the Supreme Court put it in *Buckley v.*

Valeo,[179] the draftsmen of the Constitution, "saw that a hermetic sealing off of the three branches of Government from one another would preclude the establishment of a Nation capable of governing itself effectively." Judicial independence cannot be absolute, and historical examples bear this out. The rule-making power is one of the most important examples of practical necessity dictating that a twilight area be created where activities of the separate branches merge.[180]

In the end the question of whether the legislature or the courts or both should possess the rule-making power comes down to a policy question where a series of arguments such as the following must be weighed and balanced:

1. The federal judiciary has an unprecedented history of judicial independence from the other branches. Arguably, a crucial part of that independence lies in a power to formulate the rules by which cases are to be litigated and processed since the process of litigation often has a crucial effect on determination. For courts to surrender this power to the legislature is to give up a crucial aspect of their duty to fairly determine cases and controversies.

2. Courts have an intimate knowledge of the need for particular rules to govern court processes not possessed by the legislative branch.

3. The legislature has the prerogative to determine questions of a general nature not bound by the particular confines of a judicial dispute under the Constitution and laws. Rule-making must inevitably be classed as such a legislative prerogative. The legislature has this prerogative because it is far closer to the people's wishes than the courts; leaving rule-making solely in the hands of the courts is to invite the kind of court abuses that arose in early nineteenth-century England.

54

4. The legislature, unlike the courts, possesses sufficient detachment and distance to be able to evaluate needs for rules to alter judicial procedures; courts are so intimately bound to the status quo that they cannot obtain the breadth of view necessary to impose occasional reforms.

5. Court procedure will inevitably affect practical substantive rights, including those adopted by Congress. For example, making court practice more speedy, cheaper and simpler will make it easier for plaintiffs to vindicate their substantive rights. Where remedies are difficult to obtain and there is no effective remedy, there is no effective right. The legislature must ensure that the substantive rights it provides can be protected.

Each of these arguments is postulated in absolutist terms; we turn now to the historical practice of rule-making to demonstrate that rigidity of position has not prevailed.

II:D. Historical Origins of the Rule-Making Power of Federal Courts

As outlined above, the rule-making power of the federal courts has its roots in the practices of English courts and the strong American tradition of an independent judiciary. But its first embodiment was in legislation: the Judiciary Act of 1789 and the Process Acts of 1789, 1792, and 1793.[181]

II:D:1. The Judiciary Act of 1789

Much of article III of the Constitution was not self-executing, but required extensive congressional legislation. In the beginning there was the Judiciary Act of 1789.[182]

Section 17 of the Act empowered the several federal courts to establish their own rules "for the orderly conducting [of] business," but the Act itself limited the extent of the courts' discretion to make rules by setting forth a number of basic procedural requirements. As drafted by the Senate Committee for Organizing the Judiciary, the Act set forth the powers of the federal courts to issue writs, and to grant new trials in jury cases where new trials had been granted in courts of law. It also outlined discovery procedures, the methods of proof to be employed at trial, and procedures for taking depositions. A jeofails section to secure decisions based on the merits rather than on legal form, and a provision that actions would not abate in the event of death of one party or the other but be continued by executors or administrators was also adopted.[183]

The final version of the Act modified a number of these provisions of the committee draft. The committee discovery procedures were based on chancery proceedings, and a concern over jury usurpation and self-incrimination led to elimination by the Senate of a requirement that a defendant be required to disclose under oath his knowledge of the cause. Books and papers remained discoverable.[184] A Senate amendment required circuit courts to set forth findings of facts in equity and admiralty cases.[185] To some extent the legislative revisions of the committee's draft expanded the courts' rule-making powers. The Senate liberalized the jeofails section by enabling the courts to allow either party at any time to amend any defect in process or pleadings upon such conditions as the courts *"shall in their discretion, and by their rules prescribe."*[186] The House protected the procedural rights of criminal defendants by limiting this section to civil cases.[187]

The Act as a whole recognized, despite the detailing of basic procedures, that courts would play a crucial role in shaping the law through common law judicial decision. For example, concerning writs, the Act's direction that all writs, including nonstatutory writs, be issued in accord with "principles and usages of law," underlined the courts' inherent procedural and rule powers. Similarly, the amended jeofails section authorized courts to make judgments "according as the right of the cause and matter of law appear to them."[188]

Although in retrospect many of the Act's provisions appear as a brilliant selective amalgam of varied state procedures, contemporary opinion was uneasy over some of the Act's imperfections. Madison, for example, hoped that the judges would subsequently reconsider and revise the act.[189] His view probably reflects a contemporary attitude that implied power to design court procedures rested in the courts as well as Congress.

II:D:2. The Process Acts

"An Act to regulate Processes in the Courts of the United States" emerged late in 1789 from the same committee and Congress that had brought forth the earlier Judiciary Act. Although the Process Act aimed to establish the forms of process in the federal courts, through its subsequent revisions it had an impact on the powers of courts to set rules. The 1789 Process Act contained no direct discussion of rule-making by the courts and was drafted as a temporary expedient. The role of the judiciary in determining the forms of process was recognized when efforts to revise the 1789 Act began; the Committee for Organizing the Judiciary in 1790 requested the Justices of the Supreme Court "to furnish them with such Remarks as should occur to them in this Business." The committee hoped that the Justices

would prepare a Bill or afford them some aid in doing it, [but the Supreme Court did not] . . . as the Judges from the Southern States were not present, those who attended, not being acquainted with the Forms used at the Southward, were unwilling to propose such as would be used in all the States and thought it prudent not to do it at present.[190]

Congress undertook revision of the 1789 Process Act in 1792. As revised by the House, all proceedings in admiralty were to be according to the civil law, subject to such alterations and additions as the courts "shall in their discretion deem expedient," or to such regulations as the Supreme Court should think proper from time to time to prescribe to any circuit or district court.[191] The Senate version of the bill extended the scope of judicial rule-making to proceedings at common law and equity as well as to admiralty; thus equity, common law, and admiralty proceedings were "subject . . . to such alterations and additions as the [federal] courts respectively shall in their discretion deem expedient, or to such regulations as the supreme court of the United States shall think proper from time to time by rule to prescribe to any circuit or district court concerning the same. . . ."[192]   It was the Senate provision that was eventually enacted.

The Supreme Court moved promptly to effectuate this grant of rule-making power, for the August 8, 1792, entry in the minutes of the United States Supreme Court shows the following:

> The Chief Justice . . . state[s] that—This Court consider the practices of the Courts of Kings Bench and of Chancery in England, as affording outlines for the practice of this Court and that they will, from time to time, make such alterations therein, as circumstances may render necessary.[193]

The Supreme Court, in adopting rules of practice for cases before it, clearly envisioned that its rule-making power extended to common law and equity actions.

In 1793 the courts' rule-making power was again considered. To a Senate bill concerning the structure of the circuit courts, the House added a section which aimed to supplement the rule-making provisions of section 17 of the Judiciary Act of 1789 and the Process Act of 1792. The section aimed to shift the power to make rules for practice from all of the federal courts to the Supreme Court alone. The Senate apparently considered this too great a departure from previous policy and changed the language of the section to place rule-making power in "the several Courts of the United States."[194]   The provision, as enacted, read:

> . . . it shall be lawful for the several courts of the United States, from time to time, as occasion may require, to make rules and orders for their respective courts directing the

returning of writs and processes, the filing of declarations and other pleadings, the taking of rules, the entering and making up judgments by default, and other matters in the vacation and otherwise in a manner not repugnant to the laws of the United States, to regulate the practice of the said courts respectively, as shall be fit and necessary for the advancement of justice, and especially to that end to prevent delays in proceedings.[195]

The 1793 law continued the tendency of the 1792 Process Act to relax legislative control over rule-making and to expand the court's powers in that area. Although Congress retained the power to intervene to formulate rules of practice and procedure, as indicated by the phrase requiring the rules to be "in a manner not repugnant to the laws of the United States," the practical authority to formulate rules shifted to the courts.

II:D:3. Subsequent Laws

The placement of basic rule-making power in the courts in the Process Act of 1793 was sweepingly reaffirmed in an 1842 law:

That the Supreme Court shall have full power and authority, from time to time, to prescribe, and regulate, and alter, the forms of writs and other process to be used and issued in the district and circuit courts of the United States, and the forms and modes of framing and filing libels, bills, answers, and other proceedings and pleadings, in suits at common law or in admiralty and in equity pending in the said courts, and also the forms and modes of taking and obtaining evidence, and of obtaining discovery, and generally the forms and modes of proceeding to obtain relief, and the forms and modes of drawing up, entering, and enrolling decrees, and the forms and modes of proceeding before trustees appointed by the court, and generally to regulate the whole practice of the said courts, so as to prevent delays, and to promote brevity and succinctness in all pleadings and proceedings therein, and to abolish all unnecessary costs and expenses in any suit therein.[196]

The development of particular sets of federal rules will be explored below.

II:E. Evolution of Present Federal Procedural Rules

Currently, the Supreme Court and the federal courts are given general authority to establish rules for the conduct of their own business by section 2071 of title 28 of the United States Code. The Supreme Court possesses specific authority to prescribe rules of procedure for lower federal courts in bankruptcy cases,[197] in other civil cases,[198] and in criminal cases,[199] and to revise the rules of evidence.[200] This current statutory framework is relatively young.

II:E:1. Federal Equity Rules

Equity was viewed as distinct and separate from law. When Congress, in the Process Act of 1789, first faced the problem of how federal courts were to deal with equitable doctrines, it enacted a temporary provision that "the forms and modes of proceedings in causes of equity . . . shall be according to the course of the civil law."[201] The Process Act of 1792 revised this formulation, providing that the forms of equitable process were to be according to the principles and rules of equity "as contradistinguished from courts of common law."[202] Added to that provision, as already noted, was a proviso that made it

subject however to such alterations and additions as the several courts respectively shall in their discretion deem expedient, or to such regulations as the supreme court of the United States shall think proper from time to time by rule to prescribe to any circuit or district court concerning the same.[203]

Because equity was largely undeveloped in the states, section 34 of the Judiciary Act of 1789—the "Rules of Decision Act"—was not made applicable to federal equitable actions. As a result, equity procedure developed without substantial pressures toward conformity with state procedures, and the Supreme Court possessed considerable freedom in equity rule-making.

The Court, however, waited to exercise its power until 1822 when it issued thirty-three equity rules.[204] In 1842, the Supreme Court issued a revised set of ninety-two equity rules.[205] Neither the 1822 nor 1842 equity rules embodied a comprehensive codification but, rather, they served to supplement and clarify details of traditional chancery practice.

Long after the 1842 rules became obsolete, the Supreme Court undertook a systematic revision, culminating in the Equity Rules of 1912.[206] In 1915 Congress intervened in the rule-making process to provide that equitable defenses were available in legal actions and that equitable actions were transferable to states as legal actions and vice-versa. Although the 1912 Equity Rules generally were considered successful, the Supreme Court was criticized for failing, either by case decision or amendment, to clarify the rules as disputes arose.[207] Finally, in 1938, long after New York had joined law and equity in the Field Code, law and equity were merged in the federal courts by the superseding Federal Rules of Civil Procedure.[208]

II:E:2. Admiralty Rules

Just as equity developed in England under the separate institutional auspices of chancery courts, admiralty developed under the separate judicial roof of the admiralty courts. Largely because of its history, admiralty, like equity, was conceived of by the first Congress as distinct from the common law, requiring its own unique legal language and procedures.

The Process Act of 1789[209] provided that admiralty proceedings "shall be according to the course of the civil law." This stopgap measure was replaced by the Process Act of 1792 with a provision that admiralty proceedings were to be "according to the principles, rules and usages which belong . . . to courts of admiralty . . . , as contradistinguished from courts of common law."[210] The same allowance for rule-making by courts that attached to the equity provision applied to admiralty.

From 1792 until 1842, the Supreme Court failed to exercise its admiralty rule-making power and left the field to conflicting rules developed by district courts. With the impetus of the reaffirmation of the rule-making power in the Act of August 23, 1842,[211] the Supreme

Court issued forty-seven admiralty rules in 1844.[212] Like the equity rules of 1822 and 1842, the admiralty rules were not a comprehensive codification but were clarifications of, and additions to, traditional admiralty practice. The 1844 rules, frequently amended, remained in effect until 1921, when they were superseded by an extensive revision.[213] In 1966, admiralty procedure was merged with civil procedure[214] and the Federal Rules of Civil Procedure are now applicable to admiralty as well as civil cases.[215]

II:E:3. Bankruptcy Rules

Article I, section 8 of the Constitution grants to Congress power "To establish . . . uniform laws on the subject of bankruptcies throughout the United States." Current bankruptcy laws are a combination of an Act of July 1, 1898,[216] a major revision undertaken in 1938,[217] and approximately one hundred amendments to these acts.[218]

Shortly after passage of the Act of July 1, 1898, the Supreme Court formulated rules for bankruptcy procedures.[219] The rules were frequently amended and were systematically revised in 1939.[220] They were revised again in 1974 pursuant to proposals of an advisory committee.[221]

II:E:4. Federal Rules of Civil Procedure

Section 34 of the Judiciary Act of 1789 provided "That the laws of the several states, except where the constitution, treaties, or statutes of the United States

64

shall otherwise require or provide, shall be regarded as rules of decision in trials at common law in the courts of the United States in cases where they apply."[222] This Rules of Decision Act left it unclear whether state law was to govern procedure. It was remedied by the subsequent Process Act of 1789, which required federal courts to follow, in actions at law, state procedure in effect at the time of the passage of the act.[223] The Process Act of 1792 ratified this provision but, as already noted, made it subject to the same rule-making power in the Supreme Court and lower federal courts that applied in equity and admiralty cases.[224]

Whereas the Judiciary Act of 1789 dictated a dynamic conformity for substantive law, the Process Act of 1792 imposed a static conformity for procedural law, save for any alterations made by courts' exercise of their rule-making powers. Static procedural conformity became increasingly awkward as states shifted away from 1789 procedures and as new states were added to the union. Although these problems could have been alleviated if courts had exercised their rule-making powers, the courts refrained from doing so.

Faced with the reluctance of the courts to adopt procedural rules for actions at law, Congress occasionally enacted statutes to reduce some of the problems with static conformity.[225] Apparently to obtain assistance in resolving occasional conformity problems, Congress, as noted above, reemphasized and broadened the courts' rule-making powers in 1842.[226] The courts again failed to formulate rules for actions at law.

In the Conformity Act of June 1, 1872,[227] Congress replaced the rule of static conformity for procedure with dynamic conformity, and withdrew the unused rule-making power over procedures in actions at law. A proviso to the act specifically preserved for the courts power to determine evidentiary rules: *"Provided, however,* That nothing herein contained shall alter the rules of evidence under the laws of the United States, and as practiced in the courts thereof."[228] Despite the Conformity Act, distinctive federal practices inevitably emerged.[229]

A sense that necessary procedural reform could only be accomplished by court rules drafted by judges and lawyers led to a movement for uniform federal procedural rules for civil cases.[230] Professors Clark and Moore summarize the cooperative efforts of the Court, members of Congress, the bar, and the Attorney General in obtaining modern rule-making authority:[231]

The manner of passage of the act disclosed some of the ironies which seem to accompany reform movements. It was the culmination of one of the most persistent and sustained campaigns for law improvement conducted in this country, one sponsored by the American Bar Association since 1912, under the militant leadership of Mr. Thomas W. Shelton and his Committee on Uniform Judicial Procedure, and supported by some of the most distinguished of the legal profession. In fact, Mr. Shelton was able to report to one meeting of the Association (in 1916) that the bill had passed the House and Senate; but when he went to Washington to arrange for the ceremonial signing of the act it was discovered that the wrong bill had been passed. But thereafter the bill met the powerful opposition of Senator Walsh of Montana, long chairman of the Senate Committee on the Judiciary. Finally, on the death of Mr. Shelton in 1930, the Association's Committee became less active in the support of the measure, until in 1932 the

then chairman reported his own view that uniformity in
federal actions at law was inherently undesirable, and a year
later the Committee was discontinued at his suggestion and
without opposition from the floor. But sponsorship of the bill
was then assumed by Attorney General Homer S. Cummings,
occupant of the Cabinet post for which Senator Walsh had
been originally destined. So effective was this new leadership,
that the bill became a law with surprising rapidity and
unanimity of action.

As originally sponsored by the American Bar Association,
the act authorized merely uniform rules in procedure in
federal actions at law. But in 1922 Mr. Chief Justice Taft
addressed the Association shortly before the rendering of his
decision in Liberty Oil Company v. Condon National Bank
and urged the union of law and equity in the proposed new
procedure. Thereafter there was added a second section to the
bill providing for such union, and from that time on, the bill
was pressed in substantially the same form that it had when
finally passed.[232]

Caught in the hectic pace of the early New Deal, and
assured of the Bar Association's strong approval, Congress passed the bill with almost no deliberation by
unanimous consent.[233]

The Act empowered the Supreme Court "to prescribe,
by general rules, for the district courts of the United
States and for the courts of the District of Columbia, the
forms of process, writs, pleadings, and motions, and the
practice and procedure in civil actions at law."[234] A
second section empowered the court to combine equity
and law "so as to secure one form of civil action and
procedure for both."[235] Civil rules promulgated under
section 1 were to "take effect six months after" the
promulgation of the rules by the Supreme Court; rules
unifying law and equity under section 2 were not to

67

"take effect until they shall have been reported to Congress by the Attorney General at the beginning of a regular session thereof and until after the close of such session."[236]

Chief Justice Hughes led the Supreme Court in responding promptly to the rule-making mandate.[237] In 1935, the Court issued a formal order appointing an advisory committee composed of eminent members of the legal profession.[238] The advisory committee's proposed rules received extensive evaluation and criticism through special bar and judicial committees. Its final proposals were approved with minor changes by the Supreme Court, and became effective on September 16, 1938.[239] The rules were amended four times with the assistance of the advisory committee.[240] In 1955 the Court took no action on proposed amendments, and in 1956 it discharged the Committee.

It seemed that history was to be repeated, for the Court was again ignoring the need for continuing procedural change. However, the pattern of repose was broken in 1958 when Congress ordered the Judicial Conference of the United States to,

carry on a continuous study of the operation and effect of the general rules of practice and procedure now or hereafter in use as prescribed by the Supreme Court for the other courts of the United States pursuant to law. Such changes in and additions to those rules as the Conference may deem desirable . . . shall be recommended by the Conference from time to time to the Supreme Court for its consideration and adoption, modification or rejection, in accordance with law.[241]

Acting under this directive, the Judicial Conference established a Standing Committee on Rules of Practice and Procedure in 1960, together with five Advisory Committees—on Admiralty, Bankruptcy, Criminal, Appellate, and Civil Rules.[242] The Advisory Committees draft rules, solicit comments on them, and report to the Standing Committee. The Standing Committee reports in turn to the Judicial Conference, which makes recommendations to the Supreme Court.[243] In 1965 an Advisory Committee on Rules of Evidence was added.

In *Harris v. Nelson*,[244] the Supreme Court pointed out that although Rule 81(a)(2) of the Federal Rules of Civil Procedure limits the applicability of the civil rules to habeas corpus proceedings, the habeas corpus statutes and the All Writs Act[245] give the district courts broad discretion to fashion procedures for this class of cases. Acting on this suggestion, the Judicial Conference in 1969 assigned to its Advisory Committee on Criminal Rules the task of drafting a special set of rules for this purpose.[246] These special rules have now been adopted.[247]

II:E:5. Federal Rules of Criminal Procedure

The Federal Rules of Criminal Procedure followed the civil rules. Federal criminal procedure prior to the rules, although in theory uniform, was in fact an unwieldy conglomeration of common law practice, constitutional requirements, ad hoc legislation, and references to state laws.[248]

Congress initially sought to resolve difficulties in the area of procedures after verdicts, and in 1933 authorized the Supreme Court to devise rules for this area.[249] The Supreme Court issued rules for post-verdict proceedings in 1934.[250] In 1940, Congress expanded the Court's authority to include power to draft rules for criminal proceedings prior to and including the verdict.[251] With two justices withholding approval, the Court decided to exercise this authority in 1944.[252] The resulting Federal Rules of Criminal Procedure were effective in 1946.[253] Since then they have been amended on a number of occasions.[254]

By order dated April 22, 1974, the Supreme Court made extensive amendments to the Rules of Criminal Procedure.[255] The effective date of these amendments was postponed by Congress.[256] They were ultimately enacted in a substantially revised form.[257] Congress's extensive revision of the criminal amendments was foreshadowed by its treatment of evidence, discussed *infra*. As Congressman Hungate, whose subcommittee held the main hearings, indicated, however, there is room for disagreement about whether the criminal rules were improved by congressional changes.[258] Once having started to consider them, Congress treated the Supreme Court's proposals much as any draft of proposed legislation, giving less than full weight to the substantial prior studies and the extensive work of the bodies that had reviewed them. If this is to be the pattern of the future, rule-making by the courts may become an exercise not worthy of the enormous effort required by bench, bar, and law schools.

No one, of course, can say that the Congress and its members who were particularly active in the revision were not justified in showing concern. For example, plea bargaining has been a source of much disquiet among members of the public and it was entirely proper for Congress to closely examine Rule 11(e) of the Federal Rules of Criminal Procedure dealing with plea agreement procedure. Nevertheless, on balance, one is left with the impression that insufficient weight was given to the Court's version. A presumption of validity of the rule as it reaches Congress would not unduly inhibit that legislature. Congress, it is submitted, should ask itself whether a change it seeks to make is clearly desirable before it modifies a rule.

II:E:6. Federal Rules of Appellate Procedure

In 1968, rules concerning appeals were severed. A separate set of Rules of Appellate Procedure was promulgated according to an advisory committee's recommendations. [259]

II:E:7. Federal Rules of Evidence

Prior to 1938, there had been considerable confusion about "whether given evidence questions were to be decided in accordance with the Competency of Witnesses Act, The Rules of Decision Act, the Conformity Act . . . , or some other standard." [260] The Federal Rules of Civil Procedure dealt with aspects of evidence in some twenty-one rules. [261] Nevertheless, no attempt to formu-

71

late anything like a full code had been attempted when the civil or criminal rules were developed since it was believed a separate advisory committee on this subject was preferable.[262] "Cases in the federal courts [were] badly confused."[263]

It was not until 1942 that the American Law Institute's Model Code of Evidence was formally adopted; in 1953 the American Bar Association approved the Uniform Rules of Evidence. Relying in part on the availability of these models and the need for clarification and improvement of the federal law of evidence, critics increased pressure for federal rules.[264]

A special Committee on Evidence was appointed by the Chief Justice of the United States under the program of the Judicial Conference of the United States for the study of procedural rules pursuant to authority granted by section 331 of title 28 of the United States Code.[265] The Committee concluded that the rule-making "power *conferred by . . . enabling acts of Congress*," permitted promulgation of rules of evidence.[266] It recommended that the Supreme Court adopt such rules.[267]

Subsequent history is capsulated in the Preface to the Federal Rules of Evidence Annotated by Professor Cleary for the Federal Judicial Center:[268]

In March, 1965, Chief Justice Earl Warren appointed an advisory committee to formulate rules of evidence for the federal courts. The Preliminary Draft prepared by the committee was published and circulated in 1969. 46 F.R.D. 161. A Revised Draft was published and circulated in 1971. 51 F.R.D. 315. By order entered on November 20, 1972, Mr. Justice Douglas dissenting, the Supreme Court prescribed Federal Rules of Evidence, to be effective July 1, 1973. 56

F.R.D. 183. Pursuant to various enabling acts, Chief Justice Warren E. Burger on February 5, 1973, transmitted the rules to the Congress. The Congress promptly enacted Public Law 93-12, deferring the effectiveness of the rules until expressly approved by the Congress. The Congress then amended the rules in various respects and enacted them into law. H.R. 5463, P.L. 93-595, approved January 2, 1975. The effective date of the rules is the 180th day after the date of enactment, i.e., July 1, 1975.

The rules as finally enacted are the joint product of the rulemaking process as evolved by the Supreme Court and the legislative process as conducted by the two houses of the Congress.

Details of the various drafts and controversies involving them are fully set forth in a treatise on the subject and there is no point in repeating them here.[269] There is one point that should be briefly adverted to, however, because it illustrates some of the problems of dividing rule-making power between legislature and courts.

It is generally acknowledged that many rules of evidence impinge directly and indirectly on substantive rights. Privileges are one obvious area.[270] But there are many other areas where evidence rules have a substantive impact raising delicate *Erie v. Tompkins* problems of relationships between state and federal authority, and division of control between Congress and Court on matters of substance and procedure.[271]

Particularly because Congress was in the midst of a struggle with the President over executive privileges and the rules could be construed as bearing on this dispute, there was a furor over privileges. This concern caused a delay in adoption of the rules.[272] Congress reacted by striking all the detailed rules of privilege, hoping "to leave the Federal law of privilege" where it found it.[273]

It is unlikely that it fully succeeded. For, in cases where state law does not supply "the rule of decision," Rule 501 requires that "the privilege of a witness . . . shall be governed by the principles of the common law as they may be interpreted . . . in the light of reason and experience." Since the Advisory Committee on Evidence, the Standing Committee on Rules of Procedure of the Judicial Conference of the United States, and the Supreme Court had developed the specific rules of privilege not adopted by Congress, it could be strongly argued that the rules as promulgated by the Supreme Court provide a sensible guideline.[274] In effect, the Supreme Court has rendered an advisory opinion as to current privilege law that lower courts will probably follow.[275]

For the first time since the modern rule-making statutes of the thirties, there were complaints at the hearings on the Rules of Evidence about the way the power had been exercised. Criticism centered on the lack of public participation in the advisory committee proceedings and in the lack of representation of poverty lawyers on the standing or advisory committees.[276] There also appeared to be an indication of resentment at excessive influence of a few congressmen,[277] the Chief Justice,[278] and the Attorney General, who could make their views known privately to the advisory committee. Although the huge volume of reports and letters from many committees and individuals on the published drafts that were considered by the committee demonstrate that much of this criticism was unjustified, the lack of public hearings of the advisory or standing committees may have caused some

74

frustration and unnecessary suspicion. In any event, the detailed intervention of Congress in rule-making for the first time could be justified on the ground that Congress was providing a public forum for debate.[279]

Apart from its basic policy decision on the privilege question, it is doubtful that the Rules of Evidence were sufficiently improved to have warranted all the congressional effort. Most of the changes were marginal and did not demonstrably enhance the truth-finding capacity of the courts. What many believed was the major mistake of the congressional intervention—abolition of the hearsay exception for prior identification—was subsequently rectified by readopting the Supreme Court's provision.[280]

There have been private complaints by some lawyers that they had difficulty in obtaining access to the materials relied upon by the advisory or standing committees. These materials should be readily available on request. Such grievances should not taint future rule-making procedures.

In sum, the national rule-making experience demonstrates no rigidity in doctrine or practice. Although changes in the process of rule-making have often lagged behind the need for change, lethargy more than ideology explained outmoded practice in rule-making. There are now clear signals that further changes are needed in the way rules for courts are developed.

III. Ideology Succumbs to Practicality: Courts and Legislature Both Have a Role in Rule-Making

The history of rule-making at the federal level, as demonstrated above, shows a practical accommodation between the legislature and the courts. There have been serious suggestions, however, that the legislature can have no role in rule-making. Generally this claim has been ignored by those charged with the practical task of running government. Recent history in New Jersey is instructive.

III:A. The New Jersey Experience

The New Jersey Supreme Court under Chief Judge Vanderbilt, relying on a state constitutional provision granting rule-making power to the courts,[281] took the position in *Winberry v. Salisbury*[282] that this rule-making power was not subject to legislative control; the rule would stand even if it were inconsistent with a subsequently adopted statute.

The New Jersey Court hypothesized its overruling a prior statute by rule and then the legislature readopting the statute and the court the rule, leading to an "intolerable" conflict.[283] But as Professor (now Judge) Kaplan and his associate, Greene, pointed out, the problem is not insoluble given the assumption "that court and legislature will exhibit a decent amount of mutual respect and tolerance."[284]

It is the good sense to avoid intolerable conflicts by refusing to push the notion of independent branches of government to its logical conclusion that has made it possible for our government to survive. This spirit of self-interested mutual toleration has led to the series of compromises, starting with President Washington and continuing to President Ford on the issue of executive privilege.[285] Only President Nixon failed to fully appreciate this need, and he was broken. Summarizing a thorough survey on the use of rule-making power, one commentator accurately noted: "when conflicts do arise, the courts and legislatures generally take care to avoid a constitutional confrontation by seeking some acceptable middle ground."[286]

The New Jersey position is almost unique. Other courts have taken what Kaplan and Greene refer to as "the circumspect approach"[287] in working cooperatively with the legislature.[288] The majority approach seems to be the wiser one. So long as the legislature is not seeking to destroy a court's power to act effectively, statutes should supersede rules. Unlike the courts, the executive and legislature are subject to popular will; this will, however blurred by the filter of representative democracy, should not be circumscribed unnecessarily. The Anglo-American experience with rule-making demonstrates no need for the court to have unfettered control over procedure through rule-making. Should the legislature's acts deny due process or impinge on other constitutionally protected policies, the courts reserve adjudicative powers to strike down the legislation.[289]

There has been in the last fifty years, "a growing recognition of the soundness of the policy of vesting comprehensive rule-making power in the courts, with accountability in the last analysis in the legislature." [290] No serious student of the subject would today accept Wigmore's thesis that the legislature has no power to effect judicial procedure. [291] Kaplan and Greene's wise admonition bears repeating:

Whether the subject is the controversial one of labor injunctions or the relatively neutral one of the form of a complaint or the uses of a counterclaim, it seems doubtful wisdom for a court to place itself beyond legislative control when it pronounces general rules. Even those who think that there is no need to guard against an abuse of power by the court may still sense that, in the very act of abjuring immunity from correction when it lays down a general rule, the court strengthens its moral force as an instrument of adjudication. [292]

Despite the untenability of the position, courts do still occasionally flex their muscles, making extravagant claims of exclusive power over rules. [293] The most extreme form of this position was taken by the Connecticut Court in *State v. Clemente*, [294] declaring that the legislature has no authority to make rules for the court. It is interesting that it struck down a statute granting criminal defendants discovery rights equivalent to those in section 3500 of title 18 of the United States Code, which may not have a constitutional basis under the *Jenks* case, [295] but is at least a forward-looking reform. In a thorough historical analysis of Connecticut cases, Professor Kay has termed the decision a "radical ... novelty." [296] He concludes: [297]

[T]he best safeguard to the proper balance between the courts and other departments of government lies in the responsibility of judges to exercise restraint and temperance in deciding questions touching upon their own power. In the assertion of exclusive and supreme power over matters of practice and procedure, the Connecticut Supreme Court has failed in that responsibility.

New Mexico has recently apparently also taken this extreme position. In its Rules of Evidence the Supreme Court in Rule 501 provides "Except as otherwise required by constitution, and except as provided in these rules *or in other rules adopted by the Supreme Court,* no person has a privilege. . . ."[298] Not only are prior statutory privileges abolished,[299] but the court has even apparently taken the position that subsequently adopted statutory privileges enacted by the legislature would be invalid.[300]

In the somewhat related area of legislative control over admission to the bar and bar discipline there is more of a tendency by the courts to insist on their inherent powers.[301] The reasons for this are beyond the scope of this volume.[302]

New Jersey's near fiasco over rules of evidence shows why the absolutist attitude of Judge Vanderbilt and a few others on the issue of procedural rules can not be sustained. In 1954, the Supreme Court of New Jersey appointed an advisory committee to study the Uniform Rules of Evidence that had just been approved by the American Bar Association. That committee published its report in May, 1955, comparing the Uniform Rules with existing New Jersey evidence law, making recommendations for amendments, and calling for adoption. In

October of that year the legislature appointed a special commission (subsequently known as the Bigelow Commission) to study the Uniform Rules and make recommendations. Its report was issued in November, 1956.

No further action was taken for the next several years because of a conflict as to whether the rules should be adopted by the Supreme Court, pursuant to its constitutional authority to regulate practice and procedure,[303] or by the legislature in the form of a statute.[304] At the heart of this dispute was the position taken by the Court in *Winberry v. Salisbury.*[305]

After Chief Judge Vanderbilt died, his successor, Chief Judge Weintraub, met with legislative leaders to work out a practical compromise. Pursuant to their agreement, the Evidence Act of 1960 was adopted.[306] The act included the rules of privilege and a modified Dead Man statute. It provided detailed procedures authorizing the Supreme Court to adopt the remaining rules of evidence. One provision requires the proposed rules to be presented, before adoption, to a judicial conference that includes representatives of the various courts, bar associations, legislature, Attorney General, county prosecutors, law schools and "members of the Public."[307]

As part of the arrangement between the Chief Judge and legislative leaders, the Supreme Court of New Jersey appointed a second advisory committee in 1960. The rules proposed by the advisory committee were adopted by the Supreme Court in 1964 to become effective, pursuant to the provisions of the act, in 1965.[308] The legislature then passed a series of amendments delaying the effective date to 1967.[309]

It is interesting that after enactment of the rules of evidence the New Jersey legislature set up a Permanent State Rules of Evidence Review Commission consisting of members of the legislature and private citizens to advise the legislature with respect to proposed changes in the rules.[310] The Commission's title was later amended to substitute the word "Court" for "Evidence," suggestion that the *Winberry* case was subject to further erosion.[311] In effect, New Jersey seems to be achieving much the same practical balance in rule-making as other American jurisdictions. Though commentators still talk of "complete" rule-making power not subject to subsequent action by the legislature,[312] the concept is illusory.

Nevertheless, the New Jersey courts still seem freer than most to exercise rule-making power rather than adjudicative power to meet issues that will repeatedly arise. A recent decision to control prejudgment interest by rule, despite its substantive content, extends rule-making power beyond the point most authorities would recommend.[313] Criticizing this expansionist approach, Lynch has called it "An Undue Process."[314]

III:B. Experience in Other States

By contrast with New Jersey, the courts in Florida, one of four states whose constitution does not seem to subject judicial rule-making power to legislative control,[315] have shown an extreme deference to the legislature. Lack of participation by the legislature in rule-making may have inhibited the courts from making rules that might possibly be deemed substantive. To minimize this impasse, it has been suggested that "creation of a joint legislative-judicial agency . . . would greatly enhance cooperation between two coordinate branches of government in an area of sometimes overlapping interests."[316]

Although it may appear heresy to the staunch supporters of unfettered judicial rule-making,[317] legislative control of procedure works fairly well where there are broad-based, active, well-financed agencies to prepare the necessary studies and legislation. As Judge Tate pointed out, speaking of the Louisiana situation:[318]

The writer is not convinced that . . . a transfer of rule-making powers [to the courts] is necessarily desirable at this time. On the whole, with the able ministrations of the Law Institute and Judicial Council and the respect shown by the legislature for these law-improvement agencies, statutory rule-making has worked well in Louisiana.[319]

Even the most ardent supporters of rule-making by the highest appellate court in the jurisdiction have had to concede that the power, when granted, often goes unused.[320]

Procedural reform in this country has never been the sole prerogative of legislature or court. At times the courts laid down the framework for reform, as in the late eighteenth century.[321] At other times, during a period of judicial stagnation, as in the middle nineteenth century, such legislative enactments as the Field Code became the primary vehicle for change.[322] During most of this century the striking reforms were by court rules, most notably by the various federal rules. Nonetheless, statutory changes were not uncommon; they range from business-entry exception statutes[323] to no-fault automobile-liability statutes with their complex of procedural innovations.[324]

The truth is that we move by jumps and starts and that none of our institutions can be trusted not to fall into the rut of self-satisfied approval of outworn practices. What is required is an opportunity for legislature, courts, bar, and law school to apply skill and imagination in devising new procedures to meet new problems. At the same time public deliberation to minimize adverse effects and to maximize soundness of policy and design is needed.

The American Bar Association proposals at one time recommended that in "general this rule-making function should be vested in a court of last resort, with power in other courts to make supplemental rules essential to local needs."[325] However, it is apparent that reliance on the federal model and past history rather than any doctrinaire concept of separation of powers motivated this recommendation. Judge Vanderbilt, however, took the position in his book on minimum standards that "The *complete* power is the true rule-making power both historically and analytically; a court cannot be said to be exercising rule-making power unless its rules override statutory rules."[326] This is the position he and his court espoused in *Winberry v. Salisbury;*[327] but there is no support for this rigid position in English or American legal history, and practical experience does not require it. Even in *Winberry* the New Jersey court had to rely on the particular wording of its state constitution rather than on general principles.[328]

Regardless of which legal institution initiates the reforms, public deliberation must be built into the process.

The American Bar Association in 1973 pointed out that ". . . the participation of judges, lawyers, legal scholars, and legislators in deliberations concerning the rules, the provision of staff assistance for research and drafting, and circulation of proposals for scrutiny and comment before their adoption" is desirable.[329] Most states exercising rule-making power utilize advisory groups to help draft statewide rules.[330] As noted above, even in New Jersey statutes require this kind of widely based participation before a rule is adopted.

In connection with statewide rules, the bar or other interested parties are often given an opportunity at a hearing to suggest changes.[331] In addition, it is typical to set the effective date of the rule sufficiently far after promulgation to allow objections to be raised and hearings to be held.[332] Requesting a change after promulgation, however, is much like asking for reargument; the court is reluctant to indicate that it has already made a mistake and the chance of change is slight.

Many of the states provide judicial conferences and councils.[333] The 1973 ABA Commission on Standards of Judicial Administration specifically noted that appropriate procedure should involve "opportunity on the part of members of the public and the bar to suggest, review and make recommendations concerning proposed rules."[334]

Statewide and the national federal rules are generally adopted after a body of experts is gathered to assist the courts as an advisory committee. This is one of the great strengths of the American system. The committees normally consist of judges, law professors, and practicing members of the bar. Usually a reporter, who is a law professor, gathers initial data and prepares drafts for study and revision by the advisory committee. In a number of instances there is a substantial appropriation and the staff work is of an extremely high order.

Typical is the work of the California Law Revision Commission and Judicial Council. California Rules of Evidence were adopted by the legislature upon the recommendations and drafts of the California Law Revision Commission.[335] The Commission had been assisted by law professors who prepared the necessary research studies,[336] and its preliminary proposals had been published and widely discussed[337] before being subjected to close legislative scrutiny.[338] California is one of the states where procedure is still closely regulated by a code, since it followed the Field Code of New York. Nevertheless, there are limited rule-making powers, and these are vested in the Judicial Council, made up of judges.[339] The Council apparently does not publish its rules in advance to permit criticism, and this has been a source of irritation to the bar. Local courts may adopt internal rules not in conflict with an applicable Judicial Council rule.[340]

The New York State Committee to Advise and Consult with the Judicial Conference on Practice and Procedure, which reports to the Judicial Conference, a judicial body, has modest appropriations[341] that are used to commission studies by law professors on an ad hoc basis so that the New York Civil Practice Law and Rules is under constant revision.[342] Under the New York Practice, although statewide rules are promulgated by the Judicial Conference, subject to veto by the legislature, much of the initiative for drafting changes in the statutes as well as the rules comes from the Advisory Committee.[343] The system works fairly comfortably, although it would appear to be extremely awkward.

The Commission on Revision of the Federal Court Appellate System in its preliminary report suggested that notice-and-comment rule-making be the normal instrument of procedural change and that an advisory committee representing both the bench and the bar participate in rule-making and in changes in the courts' internal operation procedures.[344] It also suggested publication of those procedures.[345]

Recognizing the need to make judicial rule-making a public process is healthy. When courts assume a legislative role, they should also assume the restraints that accompany that role. Public deliberations are a basic safeguard to insure a legislative process that is fair and informed.

Professor Leo Levin, who directed the studies for the Commission on Revision of the Federal Court Appellate system had summarized the position well some years earlier in an article with Professor Amsterdam, when he wrote:

> The whole aim of the balance of powers . . . is the creation of a scheme whereby the courts may maintain an effective, flexible and thorough-going control over their own administration and procedure, with the possibility of ultimate legislative review in cases where important decisions of public policy are necessarily involved. This is the aim of safe efficiency: immediately practical, fundamentally democratic.[346]

This has been the position of the Supreme Court and Congress in the field of rule-making.

IV. Reforming National Rule-Making

*IV:A. Congressional Power to Delegate
and Modify Terms of Delegation*

At one time it might plausibly have been argued that delegation of such nonadjudicative functions to the courts as rule-making was improper. History has, as already noted, made that argument untenable.

Writing for the Supreme Court in *Wayman v. Southard,*[347] Chief Justice Marshall recognized the courts' rule-making powers in the course of an opinion on a related subject. Discussing delegation of legislative power, the Court found that Congress was authorized

to make all laws which shall be necessary and proper for carrying into execution the foregoing powers, and all other powers vested by this constitution in the government of the United States, or in any department or officer thereof. The judicial department is invested with jurisdiction in certain specified cases, in all which it has power to render judgment. That a power to make laws for carrying into execution all the judgments which the judicial department has power to pronounce, is expressly conferred by this clause, seems to be one of those plain propositions which reasoning cannot render plainer.[348]

The Court thus upheld the validity of the Process Acts. It recognized that an aspect of the Process Act of 1792 concerned the power of courts to prescribe rules for proceedings. Marshall seemed to have viewed the courts' rule-making power as descending by specific delegation from Congress rather than deriving from an independent judicial authority to formulate procedural rules.[349]

Congress's position as possessor and delegator of the rule-making power is now assumed without question by the courts. For example, the Court in *Sibbach v. Wilson & Co.*,[350] simply asserted:

> Congress has undoubted power to regulate the practice and procedure of federal courts, and may exercise that power by delegating to this or other federal courts authority to make rules not inconsistent with the statues or Constitution of the United States. . . .

Since the mid 1930s the rule-making function has been transferred through delegation almost entirely to the courts with Congress's powers over the area reduced to a monitoring status. As a result of the Court's long-standing acknowledgment of the congressional prerogative over rule-making and the extensive delegation of this function to the courts, the only questions that have arisen concerning the rule-making power involve the extent and propriety of the delegation of the power to the courts.

In the *Sibbach* case, the Court, faced with a question of the validity of certain Federal Rules of Civil Procedure, stated that even though the rules worked a major departure from past procedures, specific congressional approval was not necessary. Under the terms of the Enabling Act of 1934, Congress was given a chance to review the rules and did not do so. The Court pointed out:

[I]n accordance with the Act, the rules were submitted to the Congress so that that body might examine them and veto their going into effect if contrary to the policy of the legislature.

The value of the reservation of the power to examine proposed rules, laws and regulations before they become effective is well understood by Congress. It is frequently, as here, employed to make sure that the action under the delegation squares with the Congressional purpose. Evidently the Congress felt the rule was within the ambit of the statute as no effort was made to eliminate it from the proposed body of rules, although this specific rule was attacked and defended before the committees of the two Houses. The Preliminary Draft of the rules called attention to the contrary practice indicated by the Botsford case, as did the Report of the Advisory Committee to accompany the final version of the rules. That no adverse action was taken by Congress indicates, at least, that no transgression of legislative policy was found. We conclude that the rules under attack are within the authority granted.[351]

Justice Frankfurter, joined by Justices Black, Douglas, and Murphy, dissented, stating in part:

Plainly the Rules are not acts of Congress and can not be treated as such. Having due regard to the mechanics of legislation and the practical conditions surrounding the business of Congress when the Rules were submitted, to draw any inference of tacit approval from non-action by Congress is to appeal to unreality. And so I conclude that to make the drastic change that [the particular rule in question] sought to introduce would require explicit legislation.[352]

The two views in the *Sibbach* case, then, present a dilemma resulting from placement of the rule-making power in a tenuous balance between courts and legislature. In the foregoing sections it was concluded that historically the rule-making power has been divided between the courts and legislature. It was further concluded that practical realities make this division an appropriate one. Thus the rule-making power falls into a blurred area where precise and sharp separation of the powers of the independent branches is inappropriate. Inapplicability of strict separation of powers theory does not, however, require abandonment of the concept in the context of rule-making. Experience with general powers of legislative delegation may furnish some helpful guidelines. The administrative agencies, which assume legislative, executive, and judicial roles, furnish a useful analogy.

The traditional vision of tripartite government, at least as formulated by the framers of the Constitution, reveals Congress as the source of policy-making power. Compared to the other branches, Congress is closer to the people; since power, in democratic theory, flows from the people, Congress is properly the policy-making branch closest to the popular will. Under the doctrine of legislative delegation, Congress recognizes that it is omnipresent in every sphere where government must be active, and defers to the expertise of a delegate body, allowing it to act as a legislature in the particular area under the general policy formula dictated by Congress.

Under an outmoded theory of legislative delegation, the delegate body could not enact provisions that did not fall within the scope of the policy direction outlined by Congress. If this policy scope was exceeded, or if Congress failed in the initial legislation creating the body to outline a specific-enough policy, the delegation failed and the act of the delegate body was void.[353] Largely because the courts abused the doctrine to throttle economic and social legislation in the 1930s,[354] the theory of constitutional limits on delegation has been generally ignored or given mere lip service for several decades.[355] The courts have largely freed the delegate bodies to pursue the executive's ends.

As one commentator has recently pointed out, this refusal by the courts during the past thirty years to insist that Congress's policy-making role be preserved, coupled with Congress's own failure to assert its role, has contributed to the major governmental development of recent times: an immense expansion of the powers of the executive branch (largely carried out through a myriad of semiindependent agencies), and a corresponding drastic decline in the power of the legislative branch.[356]

It may be that the courts still have some useful role to play in a partial restoration of the former balance between executive and legislative, and that revival of the legislative delegation doctrine would be an appropriate means. Just as the delegation doctrine need not be cast aside in the area of legislative policy control over the executive, it need not be disregarded in those areas where the legislature has some degree of control over activities of the judicial branch. As we have already pointed out, the first time that the court's rule-making power was reviewed, in *Wayman v. Southard,*[357] in 1825, Chief Justice Marshall rationalized the power as a legislative delegation. That position has remained the rationale for the rule-making power.

Since the rule-making power is properly subject to legislative delegation, it follows that Congress ought to at

least have the option of establishing basic policy guidelines for court rules. Thus the mechanism of transmitting
proposed court rules for congressional approval or modification seems altogether appropriate. The process fulfills
a basic obligation under a delegation theory.

If Congress, however, insists on reviewing proposed
rules in minute detail, the whole purpose of delegation is
defeated. The reason for delegation of rule-making is to
obtain the expertise of the courts and the specialists on
the advisory committee in areas of litigation procedure
with which they are far more knowledgeable than Congress. Unless Congress sticks to the large, basic issues
contained in the rule proposals submitted to it, the ends
achieved by the delegation are undercut.

The problem, of course, is what is basic policy—as
opposed to mere detail. A few guidelines can be suggested.

First, congressional review of the initial draft of a set
of rules and the new policies they contain would generally be more appropriate than review of the occasional
subsequent amendments, which usually only round out
an existing policy framework. Only where new amendments depart sharply from already approved policies does
congressional scrutiny seem appropriate. In this context,
congressional review of the new Federal Rules of Evidence, particularly as they affected privileges, and of
amendments to the Federal Rules of Criminal Procedure
involving plea bargaining, seems appropriate.

Second, Congress should scrutinize more carefully
rules that may have a substantive effect rather than a
technical or procedural effect. Although it was not clear
at the time of their adoption, amendments to the class

action rules of the Rules of Civil Procedure probably fall into this category.

Third, since many rules can affect substantive areas, some such rules seem more fitting for review than others. For example, if court rules would work a hardship on the rights of particular groups of individuals to obtain a full hearing or to present evidence adequately, then congressional inquiry would seem particularly appropriate. Proposed special rules dealing with habeas corpus proceedings might fall into this category, particularly since counsel may be paid from federal funds in such cases.[358] Public hearings at the drafting stage should help to reveal such areas of concern.

Obviously, any list of priorities for congressional review must be tentative. The whole rule-making mechanism, to be effective under a delegation system, depends on Congress's good will and wisdom in exercising a considered restraint. Otherwise all the expertise assembled by the various advisory committees will be almost valueless. Nonetheless, the delegation theory properly requires that congressional power to review be recognized. Historically, as discussed in preceding sections, this kind of balanced rule-making process, utilizing the two branches, has proved effective.

If delegation is possible, to whom may the power of rule-making be delegated? The delegee must be chosen in a way that makes institutional sense, that seems meet in an historical framework, and that does no violence to our conception of separation of power theory and practice. From what has already been said, it is obvious that the Supreme Court and individual courts could properly be delegated the responsibility of rule-making. So, too, could an assembly of judges such as the United States Judicial Conference or a committee or commission appointed by judges and approved by Congress. As the Supreme Court's treatment of the election campaign finance case, *Buckley v. Valeo,*[359] makes clear, Congress, though it has great latitude in delegating power, cannot ignore the proper separate roles of executive, legislature, and courts. It would, for example, seem improper today to delegate rule-making power to the president or even to an executive agency such as the Department of Justice. As we will suggest below, however, it is entirely appropriate to utilize the Judicial Conference and a standing committee and advisory committees of judges, lawyers, and others, including laypersons, in making rules for courts.

IV:B. Practical Objections to Exercise of Rule-Making Power by Supreme Court

In 1944, Justice Frankfurter opposed the adoption of Federal Rules of Criminal Procedure, stating that his opposition went not to the merits of the rules but to the Supreme Court's inability to effectively evaluate them in view of its distance from the realities of day-to-day district court trial proceedings.[360] He also objected on the ground that it was undesirable for the Supreme Court to appear, through the issuance of rules, to be prejudging issues that could come before the court in litigation. Justice Black also opposed, without explanation, adoption of Federal Rules of Criminal Procedure. Justices Black and Douglas objected to the rule-making process in general, as well as to particular sets of rules.[361] In opposing amendments to the Federal Rules of Civil Procedure adopted in 1963 and recommending that rule-making be by the Judicial Conference, they stated:

...We believe that while some of the Rules of Civil Procedure are simply housekeeping details, many determine matters so substantially affecting the rights of litigants in lawsuits that in practical effect they are the equivalent of new legislation which, in our judgment, the Constitution requires to be initiated in and enacted by the Congress and approved by the President. The Constitution, as we read it, provides that all laws shall be enacted by the House, the Senate, and the President, not by the mere failure of the Congress to reject proposals of an outside agency. . . .

Instead of recommending change to the present rules, we recommend that the statute authorizing this Court to prescribe Rules of Civil Procedure, if it is to remain a law, be amended to place the responsibility upon the Judicial Conference rather than upon this Court. . . . It is . . . [the Conference and its committees] who do the work, not we, and the rules have only our imprimatur. . . . Transfer of the function to the Judicial Conference would relieve us of the embarrassment of having to sit in judgment on the constitutionality of rules which we have approved and which as applied in given situations might have to be declared invalid.[362]

The Supreme Court responded to Justices Frankfurter, Douglas, and Black with the comment that "The fact that this Court promulgated the rules as formulated and recommended by the Advisory Committee does not foreclose consideration of their validity, meaning or consistency."[363]

The argument that the Court is completely free in fact to reconsider the rules it adopted legislatively when they come before it judicially is not supported by the history of judicial review of rules. For example, in *Hanna v. Plumer*,[364] the Court held, construing the *Erie v. Tompkins* effect of Rule 4(d)(1) of the Federal Rules of Civil Procedure, that the rule was not only constitutional but within the congressional mandate embodied in the Rules Enabling Act. Emphasizing the point, it noted that the *Erie* Doctrine had "never been invoked to void a Federal Rule."[365] The Court relied in large part on the fact that the Court had adopted the rule itself and that Congress had allowed it to become effective. But the particular issue posed in the case was never considered by either the Court or Congress in the context of a firm, factual situation during the course of the rule-making process. The Court stated:

When a situation is covered by one of the Federal Rules, the question facing the court is a far cry from the typical, relatively unguided Erie choice: the court has been instructed to apply the Federal Rule, and can refuse to do so only if the Advisory Committee, this Court, and Congress erred in their prima facie judgment that the Rule in question transgresses neither the terms of the Enabling Act nor constitutional restrictions.[366]

This is hardly the kind of neutral approach that should be expected of the Supreme Court.

Despite the fact that the rule was in a sense "outcome-determinative," for it affected the particular decision in the case and might well have an impact on the class of cases involved, the critical question in *Hanna* of whether the issue was one of substance or procedure had, in effect, already been determined by adopting the rule since the Court had legislatively determined that it was one of procedure. There was, in short, a presumption of the constitutionality of the rule controlling the characterization of substance and procedure in individual cases.

Hart and Wechsler summarize this dilemma by commenting that, "To a significant extent, Hanna remits important *Erie* issues from the Court as a decider of cases to the Court (and its advisers) as a promulgator of rules."[367] This means, of course, that the Court may have taken a position on *Erie* issues that, as Justice Harlan points out in his concurrence in *Hanna,* involve constitutional questions basic to the federal system[368] without either the traditional legislative or adjudicative protections.

Hanna was strongly relied upon by the advisory committee drafting the Federal Rules of Evidence, and many commentators concluded that whatever the Court wished to do in the way of adoption of Federal Rules of Evidence and privileges it could do.[369] It may legitimately be asked whether the result in *Hanna* would have been the same if a district court had adopted such a rule so that the Supreme Court's own power, prestige, and wisdom had not been at stake.[370]

Hanna's force has not been reduced by congressional revision of the Federal Rules of Evidence. Congress did not overrule *Hanna.* It merely determined on grounds of desirable public policy, that rules of privilege should not be adopted through rule-making at this time.

Not much has been gained by the Supreme Court's contribution to improvement of the rules except through the lending of its name. In general, its changes in the rules forwarded to it have been miniscule.

Perhaps the most well-known of the Supreme Court's own infrequent changes in rules proposed to it was the elimination of the work product rule proposed in 1946 by the Advisory Committee on the Civil Rules.[371] Since the issue was before it in a pending case, "the Court declined to adopt the amendment, preferring to handle the matter by decision,"[372] in *Hickman v. Taylor*.[373] The *Hickman* doctrine was ultimately embodied in Rule 26(b) of the Federal Rules of Civil Procedure by the 1970 amendments.[374]

Another significant impact on the substance of the rules occurred in connection with its action on Rules of Evidence. The assumption of members of the Advisory Committee on Evidence was that the Supreme Court returned for further study the first proposals for the new Rules of Evidence transmitted to it by the Judicial Conference in large part because it was split 4-4 on the definition of a "representative of the client" in the area of attorney-client privilege. It was unable to either adopt or reject the corporate "control group" test in *Harper & Row Publishers, Inc. v. Decker*.[375]

The next version forwarded to the Supreme Court and adopted by it omitted this definition.[376] Particularly in the attorney-client privilege area where complex policies of privilege, ethics, and regulation meet, legislative pronouncements are difficult; certainly the Supreme Court should not be inhibited from drawing delicate lines by the general language of the rules.[377]

Apparently in both the work product and privilege areas contemporaneous litigation had sharpened the

Court's awareness of the subtleties of the problems. This made it less anxious to adopt general rules.

On the other hand, more can be lost by Supreme Court participation in rule-making than the loss of the independent judgment when the Court sits to hear appeals, a loss that has already been described. There is a tendency for the Court's deliberations as a rule-making body to be shrouded in secrecy. And, of course, the legitimacy of rules, like any legislation, stems in large part from the public access to the reasoning of the decision-makers. An example of the Court's failure in this regard occurred when the Court reshaped the informer privilege as outlined in the Rules of Evidence to favor the government's position. There is a suspicion that it was influenced by the Attorney General's views, which had not been fully accepted by the advisory committee,[378] but no explanation for the change was given. The impenetrability of the Court's decision process contrasts with congressional procedures, where hearing, reports, and floor debates generally permit the reasons for important changes to be deduced, if they are not made explicit in reports.

In the long run a more serious loss than the loss of some legitimacy for the rules may be at stake. Congressional criticism of rules creates an unnecessary conflict between the Court and Congress and reduces the Court's prestige and reputation for unbiased independence. This conflict was brought home to members of the Advisory Committee on Rules of Evidence and the Judicial Conference's Standing Committee in a fairly concrete way. While Congress was considering the Rules of Evidence, these committees met together to respond to various

101

changes Congress was considering. A number of us felt that some of the proposed modifications made sense and we were prepared to inform the legislators involved of this fact. Word was passed to us, however, that the Chief Justice believed that it was our duty to defend before Congress any rules promulgated by the Supreme Court. It was a disquieting moment. We switched from an objective analysis of the merits of specific proposals to a bland defense of the Supreme Court's rules and a weak rejection of those of the congressional committee.

To summarize, at the present time, the disadvantages to Supreme Court rule-making seem greater than the advantages.

First, since the members of the Supreme Court have less day-to-day experience with details of lower court practice than any other judges, they are less apt to be able to exercise their judgment effectively and in the main must closely follow recommendations made to them.

Second, the Court's prior adoption of the rules substantially reduces the Court's ability to independently evaluate whether rules are consistent with federal statutes and the Constitution when these issues are raised on appeal. As a result, important issues do not receive the constitutional scrutiny they merit.

The flexibility of the Supreme Court in balancing a variety of constitutional, statutory, and other factors is inhibited by its having adopted rules. The point is illustrated by Chief Judge Lumbard's forceful argument that rule-making rather than *Miranda* should have dealt with in-custody interrogation.[379] He argued: rules rather than a constitutionally based decision might have been amended more easily; some experimentation with other techniques was desirable and rules would have permitted this; rule-making would have permitted full consideration of the views of other federal and state judges, members of the bar, law enforcement officers, and others; the American Law Institute's then eighteen-month-old drafting project on a prearraignment code could have provided a more sophisticated draft covering more of "the many problems which follow in the wake of so complete a break with the past";[380] and promulgation with an effective date in the future could have permitted planning of police and others without frustrating prosecutions in process.

All these advantages relied upon by Judge Lumbard would accrue if the rules were adopted by another judicial agency, without limiting the flexibility of the Supreme Court to depart from the rules where it believed the Constitution required different state standards or where congressional statutes or the Court's power to control lower federal courts required modifications to meet special problems not foreseen or adequately dealt with by the rule-makers. The Court would not be inhibited in criticizing the rules since it did not promulgate them. The Court's input into the complex of law making through cases could, when desirable, be reflected in subsequent amendments to the rules. The Court would stand above and apart from lawmaking, doing what it does best, adjusting the law to a complex of constitutional provisions, statutory amendments, rules, prior decisions, and changing societal and institutional needs in the light of particular problems presented in an adversarial setting. There is too much risk when the Supreme Court adopts rules almost blindly, as it must, that it will needlessly sap two of its great institutional strengths—flexibility and dispassionate uninvolved decision-making.

Third, in instances such as those involving the privileges in the Proposed Rules of Evidence, which were rejected by Congress, in effect the Court has given an advisory opinion that will guide the lower courts—an unnecessary departure from theoretical judicial doctrine.

Finally, the public criticism at congressional hearings of the Supreme Court's exercise of rule-making power makes the present system costly to the Supreme Court as an institution. It is not difficult to understand why Justices Frankfurter, Black, Douglas, and Warren, among others, have preferred to see the rule-making authority elsewhere than in the Supreme Court.

Justice Warren, as well as Justices Douglas and Black, preferred the Judicial Conference as the repository.[381] Shifting peripheral duties, such as rule-making, should be particularly attractive at a time when the adjudicative workload that the Supreme Court is carrying is so enormous that proposals for substantial structural changes are being considered.

The underlying point remains that the Supreme Court as a body has never challenged Congress's basic authority over rule-making, even though the execution of this function has increasingly fallen to the courts. Historical precedent also makes it clear that Congress possesses the power to modify the way the rule-making authority is exercised. Thus, there are no consitutional impediments to making improvements in the system. The only consideration that should dictate the nature of changes are practical ones.

IV:C. Proposals for Modifications of National Rule-Making Process

The current American solution to the placement of rule-making power resembles the British solution: authority is balanced between legislative and judicial branches, with fundamental responsibility delegated to a judicial offshoot, the Judicial Conference (and its attendant advisory committees), which is comparable to Britain's Rule Committee. The Conference draft is theoretically subject to revisions by the Supreme Court, and Congress reserves power to set aside or revamp any provisions. This is a relatively recent division of responsibilities that has worked fairly well, but now shows some signs of weakness. Since practical rather than ideological considerations have determined how the matter is to be dealt with, Congress and the courts should not hesitate to consider further modifications in the process. No tradition or vested interest prevents a fresh look at the matter.

One of the great advantages of giving the rule-making power to the Supreme Court was that its great prestige stood behind the rules. Perhaps this prestige induced state courts to follow federal rules. But, it is more likely that the decision to follow federal practice was based upon the merits of the model. It can also be assumed that in the future the advisory and other committees that draft federal practice will be no less sensible than they have been in the past. The Supreme Court's role in the process is also irrelevant to the extent that many states are wedded to federal practice in order to provide uniformity.

There is, it is plain from the discussion to this point, considerable merit in criticisms of present rule-making procedure. Professor Lesnick, for example, summarizes his objections as follows:

The lack of sufficiently widespread input by all segments of the legal profession and by the public, as a result of the procedures by which the Judicial Conference and the advisory committees reporting to it draft rules and recommend them to the Supreme Court.

The relative unrepresentativeness of the advisory committees and the excessive centralization of authority in a single individual, the chief justice.

The inappropriateness of utilization of the Supreme Court as the official promulgator of the rules.

The lack of a meaningful mode of congressional review that does not undermine the rule-making process itself.[382]

Based on his critique and my own I support most of his first three recommendations:[383]

1. Judicial Conference procedures should be made more open and should be published.

2. The composition of the advisory committees should be more representative. . . .[384]

3. The assignment of a rule-promulgating role to the Supreme Court is unwise and inappropriate and should be re-examined.

He also makes a number of suggestions regarding Congress's role. He would double the ninety-day period of delay to permit Congress a more realistic amount of time to consider the rules.[385] Although Congress does need more time than it now has for review of rules, it is desirable to limit the period so that necessary changes will not be put off indefinitely while Congress addresses itself to more pressing matters. Moreover, he is on sound ground in objecting to the present system permitting one house alone to block changes. This creates "a real danger of a prolonged stalemate. . . ."[386]

Rules of evidence do not take effect until 180 days after they have been reported by the Chief Justice.[387] Either house may reject or defer an amendment.[388] Any amendment "creating, abolishing, or modifying a privilege," must be approved by act of Congress and thus will go to the president for signature.[389] Other rules become effective 90 days after being reported to Congress and require an act of Congress for deferral or modification,[390] except that criminal rules on "Procedure after Verdict," need not be reported to Congress.[391] There is no persuasive reason why all this national rule-making power should not be exercised in the same way and be subject to the same control by Congress.

Professor Lesnick's last point seems more doubtful if it implies detailed revisions of all proposed rules.[392] It is

4. A workable mode of genuine congressional review needs to be devised.

Generally, I believe the review by Congress should avoid unnecessary attention to procedural details of court practice.[393] Congressman Hungate admitted that the "current Federal Rules of Criminal Procedure . . . , as amended by Congress, . . . is less desirable than the rules as first promulgated by the U.S. Supreme Court."[394] So long as the rules themselves are adopted by a court body with full legislative protection, including public participation in hearings, full notice of all changes, and adequate justification of rule-making decisions,[395] there is no need to repeat hearings and delay needed improvement in court practice. If a matter becomes important enough for congressional intervention, legislation is probably desirable, with formal participation by both houses and the president. An example is the Speedy Trial Act of 1974 adopted after Rule 50(b) had dealt with the same problem.[396] Since no speedy trial rule will work unless the courts are granted the personnel to make the rule a reality, congressional expression on the policy of speedy trials was desirable. It is noteworthy, however, that though Congress was quick to embrace the concept of speedy trials, it has been slow to supply the new judges needed to effectuate the policy.

Apparently, the present Chief Justice favors more effective coordination between the advisory committee, the Supreme Court, and congressional committees. For example, Judge Thomsen in presenting the proposed amendments to the new criminal rules to the House subcommittee pointed out:[397]

I am authorized to say that the Chief Justice, as well as members of the standing committee, believe it would be wise to have a closer relationship with members of the appropriate congressional committees while proposed rules are being discussed by the several advisory committees and by the standing committee of the Judicial Conference. Perhaps a member of your committee and a member of the appropriate Senate Committee, or someone from your respective staffs, might serve as members of the standing committee and of each of the advisory committees, or might attend meetings of those committees and comment on each proposal, as a representative of the Department of Justice sometimes is asked to do. I hope your chairman or some one or more of your members designated by him will be willing to discuss this proposal with the Chief Justice informally and with me at some mutually convenient time. I hardly need say that the Chief Justice, in his opinions over a period of 19 years, has demonstrated adherence to the concept of separation of powers and as Chief Justice he has constantly urged cooperation between the Congress and the judicial branch.

And the Chairman responded:

MR. HUNGATE. Thank you, Judge Thomsen. We appreciate the great amount of work that has gone into this and the fine quality of that work. We will certainly call to the attention of Chairman Rodino your suggestions concerning the possibility of a closer liaison between the Congress and the Judicial Conference.

If I might interject at this point, I suppose that what happens with the rules of evidence will influence the nature of the liaison. If nothing happens, and nothing happens by the first of next August, we may have learned a lesson—Congress is indeed not capable to deal with these problems. I should point out however, that until recently the Congress has, more or less by default, let slide a responsibility that does belong to it.

I do not care particularly for the suggestion that all three branches of government participate in detailed drafting of the rules, through a commission or otherwise.[398] The legislature is sufficiently involved in passing on the rules after they are proposed to it. If it were to participate in the original drafting it might be so committed as to make it less likely that it would exercise its power of review with impartiality. The executive need not be involved. It has sufficient input through memoranda and appearances it will make by its representatives, particularly the Department of Justice. If there is a bill to delay or modify the rules then, of course, the President will have his usual veto power. Ad hoc independent commissions are not a useful way to solve ongoing problems of revising practices and procedures to accord with current needs.

Another option is making the Judicial Conference of the United States the active drafter and adopter of rules. This combined role would probably not be desirable.[399] The Conference is an unwieldy and passive body heavily dominated by the Chief Justice of the United States who appoints its committees. Its controlling members are the chief judges of the courts of appeals, who achieve their status through seniority, and representatives elected by the district judges of the circuits, who serve for a short time and whose influence is transient.[400] What this body is ideally suited for, however, is the function now performed by the Supreme Court. It can do this job better than the Court and without the same hazards. Its members are in a better position than Supreme Court Justices to know what the current practice problems are and how they should be handled. At the same time, the danger of a loss of independent judgment when a rule comes before the Court for adjudication would be avoided.

This suggests that the Standing Committee on Rules of Practice and Procedure of the Judicial Conference of the United States be given legislative recognition as the body that will directly, and through its advisory committees, make the necessary studies, announce proposed changes, hold public hearings, draft the rules, and justify changes. Its recommendations should then be passed on by the Judicial Conference, which would take the place of the Supreme Court. Congress should have a veto power if both houses act within 180 days.

As a practical matter, there is now strong psychological pressure on individual advisory committee members to modify the rules in the light of what they think the Chief Justice would wish. After all, it is the Chief Justice who appointed them. The Chief Justice meets with them from time to time, and the present and last Chief Justice, who were observed by me, were most helpful and kind in attending some meetings. This expression of continuing interest and encouragement in the work was much appreciated by members of the committees. Moreover, his good will is required because as chairman of the Judicial Conference and as Chief Justice he will help shepherd the rules through the Conference and the Court and will have the necessary power and contacts, directly and indirectly, to have an impact on Congress.

Much depends, of course, upon the interests and personality of the Chief Justice. His positive interest in improving practice is healthy. Eliminating the Supreme Court's role would reduce his power somewhat, but not appreciably. As chairman of the Judicial Conference he would undoubtedly continue to have a great deal of influence, and this is as it should be.

Members of the standing committee should be appointed by the Judicial Conference. Practically this will mean delegation to a nominating committee dominated by the Chief Justice. It would be possible to subject the appointment of members of the standing committee or of its chairman to confirmation by the Senate.[401] No advantage in such confirmation is to be expected; there is no point in politicizing these offfices. There seems to be no reason to challenge the power of the Judicial Conference to appoint a standing or other committee to prepare drafts of rules. As already noted, the Conference has exercised power under grant of Congress to study the rules. Its existing Standing Committee has proposed the rules and amendments to the Supreme Court. Although clause 2 of section 2 of article II of the Constitution permits Congress to "vest the Appointment of . . . inferior Officers . . . in the *Courts of Law*,"[402] there is no reason why a committee representing all the courts, such as the Judicial Conference, should not exercise the same power in this respect as any particular "court." All the members of the Judicial Conference have been appointed by the President and confirmed by the Senate as judges. Thus, authorizing the Conference to appoint rule-making committees would merely give these judges additional duties consistent with those they have heretofore exercised. These are not "executive or administrative duties of a nonjudicial nature [which may] not be imposed on judges holding office under Art. III of the Constitution."[403]

The terms of each one of the members of the standing committee might be five years on a rotating basis. Legislation could provide for a set ratio of, say, four judges, two of them appellate and two of them trial judges, at least two law professors, and at least four practitioners.

If there are to be ex officio members of the standing committee, it might arguably be useful to have a designee of the president of the American Bar Association who would normally be a person actively involved in considering proposed changes in the federal rules for the American Bar Association. Another ex officio member might well be a representative of the Legal Services Corporation, which has recently been organized by the federal government to coordinate legal services to the poor. However ex officio appointments may lead to mediocrity, since designation by organizations tend to be for honorific reasons. On balance, the Chief Justice and Judicial Conference can be trusted to provide representation from various minority groups now that the issue has been publicly raised and brought to their attention. Moreover, open hearings during earlier stages of rule-making will permit broader participation in the process.

Using the United States Judicial Conference to appoint members may work well since the member district court judges know persons active in practice and they are more likely to respond to a request for a suggestion of names than they are to a sustained analysis of details of proposed rules. Whether the standing committee or the Conference appoints advisory committees and who should appoint reporters and subreporters are details that should be left to the decision of the Judicial Conference.

Although the Judicial Conference will probably do little more than the Supreme Court has done in connection with revisions of the proposals presented to it, there

113

is something to be said for the imprimatur of the federal judges sitting as a group. The rules are more likely to be accepted by the bench and bar, and by the states in view of the prestige of the members of that group.

It is not possible to prevent Congress from being active in rule-making if it chooses to be. The level of its activity is a function to a large extent of the personality of the chairperson and members of the Judiciary Committees and subcommittees. It would be helpful, however, if Congress recognized that it ought not, generally, involve itself in the details of rule-making, but, instead, that it should restrict itself primarily to consideration of the larger policy issues.

A public hearing by the standing committee should be required. The experience of federal agencies in rule-making is useful, even if not decisive.[404] There is no reason why the courts should have lower standards for their own rule-making than they require of administrative agencies. In recognition that important legislative considerations are involved, a full oral hearing, not merely the right to submit written statements, should be afforded.[405] The congressional hearings held in connection with the Federal Rules of Evidence furnish a satisfactory model. Such legislative hearings are "both fair and feasible" in procedural rule-making by the courts.[406]

Congressman Hungate, who probably more than anyone else in Congress was responsible for guiding the Rules of Evidence and recent amendments to the Rules of Criminal Procedure through Congress, after making note of Judge Thomsen's and Professor Lesnick's remarks referred to above, stated:[407]

It seems clear that few are entirely satisfied with the present process. The Justice Department expressed unhappiness with the way the process operated with respect to the proposed amendments to Rules 4 and 9 of the Federal Rules of Criminal Procedure. Alan Y. Cole, vice chairman of the Section of Criminal Justice, indicated in his testimony on the Federal Rules of Criminal Procedure that the section would like to become more involved in the process.

Perhaps the time is ripe for Congress to re-examine the process to determine whether or not the Rules Enabling Act ought to be amended.

From what has been said, it appears fairly clear that reexamination of the national rule-making process is desirable.

V. Local Court Rules, Guidelines, Directives, and Individual Judge's Rules

V:A. Local Rules

Individual federal courts have had rule-making power from their inception. The Act of March 2, 1793,[408] provided:

> . . . That it shall be lawful for the several courts of the United States, from time to time, as occasion may require, to make rules and orders for their respective courts directing the returning of writs and processes, the filing of declarations and other pleadings, the taking of rules, the entering and making up judgments by default, and other matters in the vacation and otherwise in a manner not repugnant to the laws of the United States, to regulate the practice of said courts respectively, as shall be fit and necessary for the advancement of justice, and especially to that end to prevent delays in proceedings. . . .[409]

But the Conformity Acts, requiring state practice to be followed, severely restricted the exercise of this power.[410]

Today, the predicates most relied upon for local rules are section 2071 of title 28 of the United States Code and Rule 83 of the Federal Rules of Civil Procedure. Section 2071 reads:

> The Supreme Court and all courts established by Act of Congress may from time to time prescribe rules for the conduct of their business. Such rules shall be consistent with Acts of Congress and rules of practice and procedure prescribed by the Supreme Court.[411]

117

Rule 83 of the Federal Rules of Civil Procedure states:

Each district court by action of a majority of the judges
thereof may from time to time make and amend rules
governing its practice not inconsistent with these rules. . . . In
all cases not provided for by rule, the district courts may
regulate their practice in any manner not inconsistent with
these rules.[412]

Inherent power has also been relied upon.[413]

Lower state courts in this country also generally have
power to make rules to govern local practice. Federal
and state local rule-making practice is similar in that
there are generally no procedures set forth in either the
statutes or the rules for rule-making by the lower courts.
In a few states the lower courts must first certify their
rules to the higher courts before they become effective.[414]

Sometimes there is informal discussion with members
of the bar and, less frequently, publication before adoption; but, generally, the lower courts adopt rules without
any systematic consultation or publication in advance.
Some of the local rules are not kept up to date nor
codified and are apparently difficult to find.[415]

One of the few thoughtful examinations of local
federal rules suggests that they are a "maze of decentral-
ized directives, encumbered by trivia and often devoid of
explanation."[416] The *Duke Law Journal* analyzed local
rules under the following heads, giving some idea of the
range of practices affected:[417]

1. Attorneys
2. Divisions within a District

3. Calendars and Motions
4. Pleadings
5. Notifications of a Claim of Unconstitutionality
6. Orders Grantable by the Clerk
7. Bonds and Undertakings
8. Depositions and Discovery
9. Pre-trial
10. Stipulations
11. Continuances
12. Dismissal for Want of Prosecution
13. Trial Conduct and Procedure
14. Impartial Medical Examinations and Testimony
15. Exhibits, Records, and Files
16. Juries: Empaneling and Instructions
17. Costs and Fees
18. Motions for New Trials
19. Appeals
20. Bankruptcy and Receivership
21. Habeas Corpus Procedure

Even this broad-ranging categorization does not complete the picture since there are diverse rules such as those noted *infra* and *supra* in connection with litigations testing their validity, and such rules as those limiting the right to appear pro se in civil rights cases,[418] providing for six-member juries in civil cases,[419] forbidding certain communications in class actions,[420] providing for expert panels,[421] outlawing use of radio and television in environs of courthouses,[422] setting out special rules of pleading and procedure in class actions,[423] requiring habeas corpus actions to be on certain forms when commenced pro se,[424] and mandating separate trials of liability and damages.[425]

Another comprehensive examination of local rules concluded that

119

the majority of district courts have, in promulgating rules, ignored the principles of simplicity . . . and uniformity which guided the formulation of the Federal Rules. At times, district courts have used their power under Rule 83 to negate specific requirements of the Federal Rules; more often, simply to escape from the arduous but essential task of case-by-case analysis.[426]

As some of the discussion below indicates, the subject matter of local rule-making continues to expand as local judges exercise their fertile imaginations to deal with perceived problems.

Summarizing the case law, statutes and rules, it has been said that the district courts may not formulate rules that are: "(1) Inconsistent with the Federal Rules, (2) Inconsistent with Federal Statutes, (3) Unreasonable, (4) Non-uniform and discriminatory."[427] Nevertheless, control of local rule-making power has been relatively ineffective.

One method of limiting local rule-making is to require reports. Rule 83 of the Federal Rules of Civil Procedure requires that local rules "shall upon their promulgation be furnished to the Supreme Court of the United States." Because the Administrative Office of the United States Courts was established after Rule 83 was adopted, other local rules are filed with it pursuant to Rule 47 of the Rules of Appellate Procedure, Rule 927 of the Bankruptcy Rules and Rule 57 of the Rules of Criminal Procedure. Only Rule 927 of the Bankruptcy Rules requires making the local rules "available to members of the Public who may request them."[428]

This reporting system provides no control at all.[429] Filing does not imply approval by the Supreme Court or by the Administrative Office.[430] Nor does central filing give effective notice to the public. Printing by private companies is relied upon by the bench and bar.[431] Although there is a private service collecting all civil, general, and admiralty rules, it does not include the local rules affecting only criminal motions.[432] There is no ready way for an attorney to obtain all local criminal rules. An attack on a local rule on the ground that a copy was not sent to the Supreme Court or the Administrative Office has little chance of success.[433] As a result, lack of knowledge of local rules may become a trap for lawyers from other districts.[434]

A second method of control is through appeals in individual cases.[435] In most instances the finality rule, limiting appeals from nondispositive orders, prevents intermediate appeals challenging local rules. Moreover, local bar associations as well as attorneys have been reluctant to cross swords with local judges by challenging their rules in litigations.[436] In one case the lawyer for one of the parties had so lost interest in the matter that the Supreme Court had to appoint an amicus to argue the validity of a local rule dealing with references to magistrates—a curious example of the failure of the adversary system in the rule-making area.[437]

A rare example of the bar's taking its courage in its hands to protest alleged overstepping by judges in rule-making is *Chicago Council of Lawyers v. Bauer*.[438] There the Seventh Circuit declared invalid, on the grounds that it was overbroad, restrictions on the comments of lawyers about pending litigation. It treated the rules in much the same way as a prior restraint statute, using normal statutory construction techniques. Approaching the matter as if Congress had adopted a statute embodying the rule,[439] it implied that the local court's power was congruent with that of Congress. Amendment to provide somewhat narrower fair press-free trial rules was suggested.[440] In an interesting concurrence Senior United States District Judge Wyzanski, sitting by designation, questioned the use by the court of appeals of what was in effect an advisory opinion construing the validity of these rules. He wrote:[441]

The nature of this proceeding raises questions whether as a matter of discretion it is consistent with the prudent exercise of discretionary judicial power under Article III of the United States Constitution, under the Declaratory Judgment Act, and under other statutes conferring jurisdiction upon the federal courts, for this court to pass judgment upon imaginary cases sometimes scorned as "a parade of horribles."
. . . .
It is plain that the complaint is not frivolous.
. . . .
Yet this action invites, in advance of a specific invocation of any rule in the form of a disciplinary or punitive action, a scrutiny of all the complex provisions of a total code of professional conduct in a broad branch of the profession of advocacy. This code has been adapted from drafts prepared after prolonged, highly competent work by professional committees of judges and lawyers of distinction and experience. They, like ourselves, of course, may have erred. They, like ourselves, were acting not in relation to immediate controversies arising out of actual conflict, but in relation to hypothetical cases which they foresaw or feared.
In short, those committees, like the District Court, were exercising a quasi-legislative function.
It might have been proper and preferable for the Circuit Council of this Seventh Circuit to have reviewed in a like legislative manner those or any other rules of the District

Court for the Northern District of Illinois. But that is not the nature of this proceeding. Here we have what purports to be an Article III "case" or "controversy." We are asked to make an adjudication. That adjudication will constitute a precedent and may have other binding consequences. Yet inasmuch as it is not addressed to specific, concrete facts it also partakes of the nature of an advisory opinion with all the dangers inherent in such speculative judgments.

Judge Wyzanski suggested that the court of appeals review the rules as a legislative body, much as it would have done under the old equity Rule 79.

Requiring approval of local rules by a superior court is a third method of control. Equity Rule 79[442] required a majority of the circuit court judges for the circuit to approve district court rules. It provided:

With the concurrence of a majority of the circuit court judges for the circuit, the district courts may make any other and further rules and regulations for the practice, proceedings, and process, mesne and final, in their respective districts, not inconsistent with the rules hereby prescribed, and from time to time alter and amend the same.

This limited form of control was abandoned with adoption of Federal Rule 83 of the Federal Rules of Civil Procedure.[443] The Federal Rules Advisory Committee considered sending the equity control rule to the Supreme Court as an alternative to Rule 83, providing for no supervision by the circuit judges.[444] Professor Moore suggests that the committee wanted to reduce "the possibility of conflict between district and circuit judges."[445]

This technique of direct higher court supervision has been followed to a limited degree, particularly in connection with attempts to obtain speedy disposition of criminal cases. [446] For example, Rule 50(b) of the Federal Rules of Criminal Procedure gives both the judicial council of each of the circuits—consisting of all the full-time judges—and the Judicial Conference of the United States input and some control over the local rules. It reads in part:

(b) Plan for Achieving Prompt Disposition of Criminal Cases.

To minimize undue delay and to further the prompt disposition of criminal cases, each district court shall . . . prepare a plan for the prompt disposition of criminal cases. . . . The district plan shall be submitted for approval to a reviewing panel consisting of the members of the judicial council of the circuit and either the chief judge of the district court whose plan is being reviewed or such other active judge of that court as the chief judge of the district court may designate. If approved the plan shall be forwarded to the Administrative Office of the United States Courts, which office shall report annually on the operation of such plans to the Judicial Conference of the United States. The district court may modify the plan at any time with the approval of the reviewing panel. It shall modify the plan when directed to do so by the reviewing panel or the Judicial Conference of the United States. . . .

Realistically, the courts of appeals control absolutely the language of the district court speedy trial plans; and, for the sake of uniformity, the plan will have its genesis in the work of a committee of judges of the Judicial Conference of the United States or of the circuit council.

Approval in advance by the circuit council means that all the sitting nonsenior appellate judges have ruled by advisory opinion that the local plan is desirable and valid. Accordingly, anyone arguing in an individual case that part of the plan is invalid will probably assume some bias in favor of the rule by the court of appeals.

In *United States v. Furey*,[447] the appellate court had before it a rule of a district court adopted as part of its Plan for Achieving Prompt Disposition of Criminal Cases. The court noted that the rule was based upon the "Second Circuit Model Plan" followed by all the districts in the circuit. Relying on this distinguished genesis and the courts' "inherent power," the court rejected the challenge to its handiwork.

Instead of relying on Rule 50(b) solely as authority, however, the court in *Furey* claimed support from power of local courts "derived independently from 28 U.S.C. § 2071."[448] It pointed out that local rules, "being within the authority of the district courts, the Supreme Court, acting in its supervisory capacity, had the power to direct that [such rules] be promulgated in order to 'eliminate technicalities and delays in criminal cases.'"[449] It then noted that Congress could have rejected Rule 50(b) pursuant to section 3771 of title 18 of the United States Code, granting criminal rule-making power to Congress:

> Yet, despite ample opportunity to invalidate Rule 50(b) as failing to meet the requirements of §3771, Congress chose to remain eloquently silent, permitting the rule to become effective. In these circumstances the words of the Supreme Court with regard to the Federal Rules of Civil

Procedure in Sibbach v. Wilson & Co., supra, 312 U.S. at 15, are apposite:

The value of the reservation of the power to examine proposed rules, laws and regulations before they become effective is well understood by Congress. It is frequently . . . employed to make sure that the action under the delegation squares with the Congressional purpose. Evidently the Congress felt the rule was within the ambit of the statute as no effort was made to eliminate it from the proposed body of rules. . . . [Footnote omitted].

As the government has failed to carry the heavy burden of upsetting a rule adopted pursuant to §3771, cf. Hanna v. Plumer, 380 U.S. 460, 471 (1965), we are persuaded by Congress' implicit approval of Rule 50(b).[450]

Of course, neither Congress nor the Supreme Court had passed on the particular local rule in question. In effect, the court of appeals was approving its own plan, which had never been reviewed by another body or tested by uncommitted judges in a case or controversy. I take no exception to the result in *Furey*. Nor do I suggest that the issue was not decided impartially and fairly. It is the process that is disquieting; courts, even more than administrative agencies, should keep as separate as possible legislative and adjudicative functions so that they will appear to be impartial.

The problem was pointed up even more dramatically in the Second Circuit when rules were adopted pursuant to the Speedy Trial Act of 1974.[451] The Eastern District of New York had adopted rules that would have excluded from the period during which a prisoner could be detained awaiting trial, delays caused by defense counsel or the prisoner. Following a plan similar to that under Rule 50(b), set out above, and incorporated in the act, this provision was reported to the Second Circuit Council. The Council rejected the district's proposal and insisted on adoption of its "model" rule. It acted privately without giving the judges or the United States attorney, who believed the "model" unsound and not required by the Speedy Trial Act, or any member of the public, an opportunity to be heard. A communication from the Chief Judge of the circuit opined that the interpretation of the act by the inferior judges and the United States attorney (who had submitted an extensive brief on legislative history to the district court judges) was without merit.[452] Should the United States attorney challenge this Speedy Trial Rule he is likely to feel that the matter has been foreclosed without a hearing; even though his extensive analysis of the legislative history and language of the act indicates a substantial issue.[453]

That the matter is not free from doubt is suggested by the steady stream of announcements on speedy trials issued by the Administrative Office of the United States Court.[454] Apart from the need for publication already noted, legal scholars can hardly comment effectively on current developments when so much of the relevant legislative and interpretative material is unknown to the public.

Legislative and adjudicative functions, when they become so intertwined, create serious dangers to the impartial decision of cases. Some formalized hearing procedures and control is desirable.

Another recent example of adoption of a local court rule without notice or an opportunity to be heard was the Second Circuit's promulgation of special training requirements for admission to its bar.[455] No announcement to the public was made in advance and no opportunity to be heard in opposition was afforded. This rule may well be in conflict with Rules 46(a) and 47 of the Federal Rules of Appellate Procedure since the appellate rules are designed to permit a national federal appellate bar ready access to all the courts of appeals.[456]

By contrast, when notice, public hearings, and an opportunity to be heard was afforded in connection with Second Circuit proposals for restrictions on admission to the bar of district courts, a serious debate developed.[457] Ultimate rejection of the proposed district court rule in the Southern and Eastern Districts of New York dramatically illustrated the value of open discussion. The Council of the Second Circuit had supported the rule and private communications from the Chief Judge of the circuit and the Chief Justice of the United States had urged the district judges to consider the proposal favorably. Without an opportunity to hear from the other side there seems little doubt that the proposals would have been quietly adopted.

Still another example of important rules adopted first and opened to public debate later are those restricting citation of "nonpublished" decisions of federal courts of appeals.[458] The various courts of appeals have adopted different rules on publication and citation that have had a serious impact on publishers of opinion as well as on advocates. Studies by one of the committees of the United States Judicial Conference were undertaken *after* the rules were adopted.[459] Although discussion of the issue on the merits is beyond the scope of this paper, national publications and the impact on national litigation obviously make some uniform approach desirable.

128

Yet no body had the authority to overrule the individual courts of appeals or to insist that they delay adoption of their rules. Even if the United States Judicial Conference had had the power, it is doubtful that it would have exercised it. With the Chief Judge of each court of appeals sitting on the Conference, normal deference would permit each Chief Judge to protect the rules of his own court.

Lack of public debate and publication of local rules before adoption is typical. As the director of the Federal Judicial Center recently indicated,[460]

local district and circuit rules are not customarily published in advance and courts do not conduct hearings thereon. I believe that the Third Circuit has published its rules for comment by the members of the bar prior to final adoption but, with this exception, I know of no advance distribution of proposed rule changes although there are bench-bar committees in some areas and perhaps some minimal contact through that source.

One of the project directors of the Judicial Center did admit: "Various lawyers we have met have expressed dissatisfaction with the court in that it did not consult the bar in advance of promulgating a new rule. This has been particularly the case where there is a bench-bar committee, as in Philadelphia, Los Angeles, and elsewhere."[461]

Mere publication is probably not enough. Members of the bar will generally not respond unless committees of the bar associations have studied the matter or the court itself appoints a committee or reaches out to invite persons who should be interested to attend a public hearing. The meetings of the circuit conferences have sometimes been used to good effect in this connection. Our experience in the Eastern District of New York, where most rules are published before adoption, is that almost no communications are received unless pointed questions are put to individuals and associations. In the Northern district of Illinois the experience has been similar.[462]

Nevertheless, the effort to involve the bar is worthwhile. In addition to valuable suggestions and prevention of inadvertent mistakes, a major advantage of involving the bar is that lawyers are more likely to accept the changes.[463]

Private adoption without an opportunity to those affected to be heard is undesirable. No rule by a regulatory agency adopted after such procedure could be permitted to stand.[464]

Lack of deliberation and public debate was apparently one reason the Court acted in *Miner v. Atlass*.[465] The Supreme Court struck down a local rule permitting depositions in admiralty cases. It stressed the necessity of mature deliberation using the rule-making power of the Supreme Court—which would be subject to congressional modification—and wrote:

The problem then is one which peculiarly calls for exacting observance of the statutory procedures surrounding the rule-making powers of the Court . . . designed to insure that basic procedural innovations shall be introduced only after mature consideration of informed opinion from all relevant quarters with all the opportunities for comprehensive and integrated treatment which such consideration affords.[466]

But such a result is rare.

130

For instance, the Supreme Court permitted a much more controversial and radical change by local rule-making when it approved six-person juries in *Colgrove v. Battin*.[467] The hint that a jury smaller than twelve, even when the parties did not so stipulate, could be forced on litigants first came in *Williams v. Florida*,[468] a criminal case. The Advisory Committee on Civil Rules, the Standing Committee on Rules of Practice and Procedure, and the Judicial Conference all agreed that a reduction in the size of civil juries from the twelve used since the republic's founding should be accomplished by statute.[469]

Despite this clearly sound conclusion that a statute with all the protection of congressional hearings was desirable before the number of jurors was reduced, local federal rules reducing juries were widely promulgated.[470] These local rules were generally adopted in the usual way by the judges behind closed doors, without open debate and full study.

It is doubtful that Congress would readily have approved such changes by statute or that it would have allowed a like change in the Rules of Civil Procedure to become effective unnoticed. Professor Moore, before the Supreme Court decided *Colgrove,* pointed out that it "would border on the quaint to suppose that the number of alternates is a matter requiring uniformity of practice under the Rules (Rule 47(b)) while the number of jurors is left to local rules."[471] The Supreme Court, however, did not agree.

Professor Zeisel has written that there is grave doubt about the statistical validity of the data judicially noticed by the Supreme Court in *Colgrove* to approve the

131

rule.[472] The matter was certainly worthy of a more effective debate than it was accorded when it was attacked as a fait accompli in litigation that culminated in the Supreme Court in *Colgrove*. Some method of holding the matter up while it was considered by a group having national responsibilities and an effective forum for debate would have been useful.[473]

The few instances where local rules have been declared invalid by a higher court involve cases where the higher court did not participate in the making of the rule. In *Rodgers v. United States Steel Corp.*,[474] for example, the court held that a local district court rule[475] empowering the district court to require prior judicial approval of communication between plaintiffs, their attorneys, or third parties, when such communication sought to encourage participation in the law suit, was outside the statutory authority of the district court, and thus subject to a writ of mandamus. The court pointed out that the rule "raises serious first amendment issues," since "important speech and associational rights are involved in this effort by the NAACP Legal Defense and Education Fund, Inc. to communicate with potential black class members on whose behalf they seek to litigate issues of racial discrimination."[476] The court found that the district court's justification of the rule as a preventative of "barratry" insufficient. Nor did Rule 83 of the Rules of Civil Procedure or section 2071 of title 28 of the United States Code permitting rules "consistent with Acts of Congress and rules of practice and procedure prescribed by the Supreme Court" justify the rule because there is "no general grant of legislative authority to regulate the practice of law."[477]

Similar issues are raised by local rules restricting comment by attorneys. They may also be overbroad and violative of first amendment rights.[478] Whether the court of appeals was right or wrong on the merits in these cases is not relevant to this discussion. What is clear is that a court which has not been implicated in the drafting and approval of the rule, is freer to give its neutral attention to the litigants before it in deciding validity. The situation is entirely different where the court itself approved the rule or guidelines.[479]

V:B. *Improvement in Local Rule-Making*

Typically, then, local rules are adopted without the aid of an advisory committee, without publication in advance, and without an opportunity for anyone to be heard before the judges act in private.[480] As Wright and Miller properly declare:

the process by which local rules are made is simply not suited for the complex and controversial subjects to which many local rules are addressed. When the Civil Rules are amended, the process is extremely careful.

. . . .

That process on the national scene is in striking contrast to the way in which local rules are made. In a few districts a committee of local practitioners is consulted but this is the exception rather than the rule. In most districts the judges consult with each other and make local rules on their own. It is decidedly the exception for the bar and the law schools to be given an opportunity to comment on proposed drafts of local rules.

. . . .

It is wholly unsatisfactory as a means of dealing with such difficult and controversial topics as separate trial of liability from damages or impartial medical examinations. Yet these, and many other equally sensitive matters, have been thought the proper subject for local rules in many districts.[481]

In one instance of this general practice of rules adoption *in camera,* the Supreme Court of New Jersey took the flat position that maximum contingent fees could be established by rule without an evidentiary hearing prior to promulgation.[482] It relied upon judicial notice and its "accumulated experience over the years."[483] However, at least the New Jersey Supreme Court did hold "an open meeting . . . with representatives of the Bar to elicit views as to the adoption of the rule."[484] Such a meeting is most unusual before local rules are promulgated.[485]

Adoption of local rules without consulting bar and law schools and without notice to the public has been properly criticized.[486] Yet, there is no practical reason why the public can not be involved.

Some courts, such as the Eastern District of New York, have adopted the practice of publishing most proposed rules in advance, sending copies to the various bar associations, and asking for comments before a specific date. Generally those comments have been sparse. My own view is that an oral hearing should be set at which testimony on the proposals will be taken, but most judges disagree with me and have not yet decided such a hearing is necessary because of the paucity of comment we have received in the past. I believe, however, that were we to set a hearing and invite specific persons to testify for and against, we could generate a reasonable debate on some of the proposals. The hearings would also give the bar a forum for ventilating other grievances and making new suggestions. For example, when this court was considering adopting its individual calendar assignment rules, a public hearing was held. It was well attended and resulted in a number of useful suggestions as well as a better understanding by both the bench and bar of the problems that the practice might generate. Some local rules are of great importance to the trial bar and to the public and ought not to be adopted in an offhand fashion. Standing committees such as those used in connection with national rules would also help generate intelligent attention to local practice.

If public participation is considered to be unwieldy, a court should at least avail itself of an advisory committee. Cognizant of the objection to ex parte promulgation, the federal judges in Iowa worked closely with the Special Committee on Federal Practice and Procedure of the Iowa State Bar Association in drafting local rules.[487]

Wright and Miller suggest that approval of local rules be required, "perhaps by the Standing Committee on Rules of Practice and Procedure or its parent body, the Judicial Conference of the United States, before they may go into effect."[488] Their alternative proposal that the power be circumscribed by specifying "those few limited areas in which local rules may be made,"[489] seems too restrictive and assumes a skill in drafting and prescience not normally available.

One advantage of having all local rules reported to a national rule-making authority is that attention to developments might suggest where national standards might profitably be considered.[490] Lacunae in the national rules may be revealed and discrepancies in local practice identified warranting elimination of conflicts for somewhat the same reason the Supreme Court attempts to eliminate conflicts between the circuits. For example, in *Miner v. Atlass*,[491] the Supreme Court struck down local rules dealing with discovery in admiralty on the ground primarily of the need for uniformity, and then adopted a discovery-deposition rule for admiralty.[492] When new national rules were adopted, as for example, the amendment making uniform the order of the parties on summation in criminal cases,[493] the national rule-making authority could consider impact on local rules, as, for instance, summation in civil cases. Differences in the six-person-jury local rules may sometimes lead to inadvertent waivers, suggesting the need for uniform national treatment.

If the Judicial Conference of the United States is given some control over local rules then the chief judge of each circuit as well as the Chief Justice of the United States and a number of district judges would, by passing on the rule, reduce somewhat their apparent impartiality should the rule come before one of them in litigation. At the appellate level the impact on any particular decision is minimized by use of panels at the court of appeals level and the entire bench at the Supreme Court level. In any court a request for disqualification would undoubtedly be honored. The risk of any possible claim by a litigant of lack of neutrality would thus be reduced to the vanishing point. Where the entire Circuit Council passes on the validity of a rule in advance, as already demonstrated, the claim of partiality may be substantial and there may be no practicable way of dealing with it.

Effective reporting and some degree of control at the national level may result in reduction of the plethora of local rules, in accordance with the original intention of the drafters of the Federal Rules of Civil and Criminal Procedure.[494] The present local rules situation has been characterized by Professor Rosenberg as degenerating into "a kind of procedural Tower of Babel."[495] Or, as Professors Wright and Miller put it, "The strong interest in developing a uniform federal procedure has been seriously compromised by the proliferation of local rules."[496]

V:C. *Quasi-Rule Directives*

The United States Judicial Conference has issued a wide range of statements to help guide lower courts, many of them of a quasi-rule-making character. They extend from disapproval of using a conspiracy indictment to convert joint misdemeanors into a felony, to suggestions of what cases should receive preferences, which ones are suitable for masters, and in which bail should be granted before and after conviction.[497]

Occasionally the directives are followed with such faithfulness that they become in effect a rule, but a rule lacking even the customary minimal procedural safeguards. In the Second Circuit a practice reducing the compensation available to attorneys appointed to represent indigent criminal defendants below the maximum level is rigidly enforced despite the fact that it was adopted without public debate or publication and at a

137

time when the cost of living was 40 percent below what it is now.[498] Perhaps because the bar was not aware of what was happening, no outcry was heard. These policy-making directives may have distinct substantive overtones.'[499]

In some state courts such as New York's, private directives from the presiding justice of the appellate division or an administrative judge control the discretion of trial judges.[500] To the extent that these directives and quasi-rules are not published, they create serious problems for the practicing lawyer.[501] He is unable to convince the trial judge to change his view and, if the directive comes from a higher court, an appeal is fruitless.

At least directives should be published. Attempts could then be made to gather, analyze, and criticize them. The same procedures of publication and hearing before adoption should be followed as in the case of other rules.

V:D. Guidelines

Courts or committees may issue guidelines that differ from rules only in the informality of their adoption. The range of topics touched upon can be as broad as rules and the influence on court activities can be as pervasive. For example, working parallel to the Second Circuit Committee on Sentencing, the Joint New York Bar Committee on Federal Sentencing Practices consisting of members of the Association of the Bar of the City of New York, the New York County Lawyers Association, the Federal Bar Council, and the New York State Bar Association, suggested\ guidelines on sentencing.[502] Presumably they would be promulgated by the Council of the Second Circuit composed of the judges of the Court of Appeals of the Second Circuit or by a committee of judges.[503] Although they would have no binding effect, the impact on sentencing would be quite substantial and would have the net effect of a rule or statute with some discretion. Widespread publicity, supporting studies, and participation by diverse sectors of the profession have already resulted in substantial changes in court practice.

My own court has adopted an extensive list of "fines" in the form of amounts that may be posted for various infractions ranging from $100 per bird for taking migratory nongame birds to $25 for advertising on certain public lands.[504] Those are "guidelines" for fines, but they will be followed. No notice or public hearing was provided.

In other instances guidelines have been issued that have the net effect, since they will almost invariably be followed, of setting policy. Even if the guideline is ignored, an appellate court will tend to be heavily influenced by it, particularly if the court participated in the formulation. For example, the deputy director of the Administrative Office of the United States Courts pointed out that the Judicial Conference made up of the Chief Justice of the United States as chairman, chief judges of each of the courts of appeals of the circuits, and an elected district judge from each of the circuits, had resolved that United States District Judges not appoint referees in bankruptcy to serve as special masters in nonbankruptcy related cases.[505]

It is no secret that there has been some dissatisfaction by trial judges with the growing insistence by judicial councils that councils have the power to control a good deal of the business and operation of the district courts. This is part of the larger problem of how federal judges shall be controlled or disciplined, and yet maintain their independence as article III judges.[506] More recently, the issue has been one reason for a move to organize district judges.[507] One Supreme Court Justice has suggested in *Chandler v. Judicial Council* that groups of judges should be less aggressive in riding "herd on other federal judges."[508]

The trend, however, is for more supervision, not less. Numerous agencies and officials have come forward in the last few decades to assist in improving court administration. The legislative history of the circuit judicial councils and conferences related in Mr. Justice Harlan's concurring opinion in the *Chandler* case indicates that the Administrative Office of the United States Courts was designed to help the courts "develop efficiency and promptness in their administration of justice."[509] The United States Judicial Center was organized to conduct studies and make recommendations with respect to the improvement of the administration of justice.[510] All these groups tend to share their expertise on the court system by issuing guidelines, drafts of rules (as in the case of the Speedy Trial Rule), and suggestions for procedures by the district and circuit courts.

This development is one that most of us interested in improving the work of the courts welcome. The net impact on the rights of litigants and attorneys may, however, be substantial. Generally this intervention results in more effective justice. Yet, in most instances, attorneys and the public are not aware of what is being done, since, typically, the decisions are brought to the attention of individual judges by letters or oral informal decisions that are not made public.

An encouraging sign that organs of court reform are beginning to recognize the need for public participation in developing guidelines, is reflected in the Federal Judicial Center's treatment of its "Recommended Procedures for Handling Prisoner Civil Rights Cases in the Federal Courts." Its proposals were marked "Tentative." The special committee that drafted the report recommended that the report "be circulated to every federal judge and to appropriate bar association groups and law school faculties."[511] Obviously, prisoner groups, legal aid-legal defender organizations, and representatives of correctional groups such as associations of guards, should be, and undoubtedly will be, given the right to be heard. The forms for orders included in the report and the suggestion that the report be kept with the judge's benchbook indicate that it will have an impact at least as great as many of the Federal Rules of Civil Procedure in controlling this kind of litigation.[512]

Much of the complex and multidistrict litigation is now conducted pursuant to a manual. It was prepared by federal judges after extensive consultation with the bench, bar, and law schools.[513]

The preliminary drafts of Proposed Court Procedure for Fair Trial-Free Press Judicial Restrictive Orders proposed by the American Bar Association's Legal Advisory Committee on Fair Trial and Free Press in July, 1975, set forth a very sensible procedure that would be useful in the adoption of guidelines.[514]

The recommended ABA procedure for adoption of standing guidelines is as follows:

1. The court drafts proposed guidelines.

2. The court makes the proposed guidelines public by distribution to the community and to state and local news media, news media organizations, bar organizations, law enforcement agencies, public defenders' offices, prosecutors' offices and such other interested persons as may come to the attention of the court.

3. The court solicits written comments and suggestions as to the guidelines to be submitted by a specified date.

4. The court schedules meetings between judges and interested persons for open discussion of the proposed guidelines.

5. The court then determines guidelines to be adopted.

6. The guidelines are publicly distributed and published broadly and generally in the community, including distribution to the persons described in paragraph 2, with a notice that they will be adopted absent a written objection to be filed with the court by a specified date.

7. If there are no objections filed, the court adopts the guidelines.

8. If objections to the guidelines or any portion thereof are filed, the court shall follow a procedure by which any persons could be heard and present facts and arguments as to how or whether the guidelines should be specifically modified.

9. After such proceeding, the court adopts final guidelines, stating the reasons for the adoption of the guidelines with specific reference to any guideline which was the object of controversy at the proceeding.

10. Review. It is recommended that some method of appellate review at the behest of interested persons without reference to a given case be afforded, since the guidelines are designed to be implemented outside the context of any particular case. Perhaps this could be accomplished by the same procedure and on the same grounds as review of local rules. Perhaps the appellate court as a supervisory court could be asked for approval or modification of these guidelines. Perhaps a judicial council would have the authority for a review. The method of review is left for local implementation.

11. The standing guidelines should be subjected to periodic review. Modification, either on the request of interested persons or *sua sponte* by the court, shall be considered by following the above adoption procedure.[515]

Although adoption of these recommendations would substantially improve present procedures for developing guidelines, I have two reservations about these specific proposals. The first difficulty is that they begin by indicating that "the court drafts proposed guidelines." It probably would be more useful, in the light of prior experience in this country, for the court to appoint an advisory committee to make initial recommendations and propose drafts. Perhaps the American Bar Association Committee believed that it was acting in this capacity and, therefore, that this preliminary step was not necessary.

Second, it will be noted that the ABA proposal Number 10 calls for approval by an appellate court. Such a review would compromise the reviewing court in the same way as prior review of rules does. When a particular case arises the appellate court may find itself unable to give full and impartial consideration to a claim that the guidelines it has already approved are overbroad.

This consideration leads me to conclude that it is unwise to require the reporting of district court rules or guidelines to the Circuit Council or of court of appeals rules to the Supreme Court, with power in the higher court to veto or revise. A procedure for reporting to the Standing Committee on Rules, with power in the United States Judicial Conference to overrule a veto would give a fair degree of protection. The delay and opportunity to resort to Congress for protective legislation might lead to more thorough consideration and possible compromises without jeopardizing the impartiality of the litigation process.

V:E. Individual Judge's Rules

Rule 83 of the Rules of Civil Procedure requires district courts to adopt local rules "by action of a majority of the judges. . . ." It has been suggested that this requirement of majority rule, somewhat restricts section 2071 of title 28 granting power to "all courts established by Act of Congress" to "prescribe rules for the conduct of their business." Arguably such a "limitation . . . promotes greater uniformity of practice within a single district."[516] If this was the intent, it has not always worked.

Particularly with the growth of individual calendars, as contrasted with general calendars, there has been a tendency for individual judges to develop their own practice. For example, one recent study points out:[517]

In addition to the ... regularly reported sets of rules which govern, *inter alia,* motion practice and calendar matters in the Southern District, at least twenty-two of the twenty-four active and four sitting senior judges have special motion and/or calendar rules with which counsel must be familiar. These special rules vary greatly and lead to some confusion among litigants. . . .[518]

The report suggests "a more readily available published edition of each judge's special rules and limited standardization."[519]

Here we are in a gray area between rule-making and the exercise of individual discretion. As to the latter category, an experienced litigator will keep book on the judges he or she may appear before, and the litigator may have a greater ability than the judge to predict the probabilities of decision on particular issues. Some variation is acceptable and, perhaps, desirable since a judge may be more efficient if he or she is comfortable with the details of his or her practice. But in some instances the divergencies seem unnecessarily idiosyncratic and a local rule-making process in which the bar and law schools had a substantial input might eliminate unnecessary differences.[520]

VI. Conclusion

VI:A. Suggested Changes in National
Rule-Making Process

1. The present division of national rule-making authority among the United States Judicial Conference and its committees, the Supreme Court, and the President has worked fairly well. Nevertheless, defects in the distribution of authority and the process utilized suggest that revision of the relevant statutes and practices is now desirable.

2. The Supreme Court should not adopt rules for any court except itself. The lack of trial experience and the heavy work load of its members give it little expertise in most of the fields regulated by rule and prevent adequate study of the issues. Although its imprimatur has the advantage of bestowing prestige on the rules, it inhibits the Supreme Court and other courts from impartially construing the rules in accord with the Constitution, statutes, and appropriate federal-state relationships. Its involvement in the rule-making process can continue through the Chief Justice of the United States—much as is now the case.

3. Congress should continue to have the power to reject any new rule or amendment by joint resolution within a limited period. Six months should suffice. Enactment of a law, which requires presidential participation, should be necessary if Congress needs more time for review or wishes to amend the rules.

4. Congress ought to restrain itself from redrafting details of rules. It should confine its involvement to the

review of substantial principles, as in its rejection of detailed federal regulation of privilege in the Evidence Rules. Changes by Congress should not be made unless they constitute clear improvements. Its detailed intervention into the Federal Rules of Evidence and the 1975 Amendments to the Federal Rules of Criminal Procedure did cause a diminution of the prestige of the judiciary as a rule-making institution. Many of the changes involved no great policy issues, but, rather personal predilections of individual members of Congress.[521]

There can, nevertheless, be little doubt of the good faith, devotion, and skill of the small group of legislators who participated in the debates leading to revision of the Rules of Evidence. Although most of the subject matter of the rules is far removed from the politician's constituency, nevertheless, Congress provides a direct link to the people who should have some way of expressing views on legislation—whether by court or Congress—if necessary, by voting to elect new representatives. This is, perhaps, only a theoretical consideration supporting continued power of Congress to intervene, but one of significance where the judges are lifetime appointees immune from popular pressure.

5. The United States Judicial Conference ought to take the place of the Supreme Court as the national rule-making authority. It has representatives of both the trial and appellate benches, and the Chief Justice of the United States, as its chairman, represents the Supreme Court of the United States. This change will not appreciably reduce the leadership role of the Chief Justice; the present incumbent's influence as leader of the courts in

improving judicial administration has generally been responsible and salutory. If an independent body of judges rather than a court is responsible for the rules, a court will be free to consider the rules impartially. As a practical matter, the Conference, through its committees, has been exercising much of the effective rule-making power since Congress, at the Conference's own request, required it to make a continuous study of the rules and recommend changes to the Supreme Court.

6. The United States Judicial Conference system of a Standing Committee on National Rules of Court Practice and Procedure and satellite advisory committees is sound. With representatives of the bar, bench, and law schools on the committees and with the tradition of law-professor reporters, a practical and scholarly orientation is successfully combined and should be preserved. Rotating terms of five years for a Standing Committee of no more than fifteen members would seem desirable. Appointment by the Judicial Conference (which means practically speaking by the Chief Justice with the advice of the Conference) should be provided to maintain the high status of membership.

Ex officio memberships are not required to ensure a broad range of representation on the committees. The Chief Justice and Judicial Conference should be expected to consult with the United States Attorney General, and such organizations as the American Bar Association, the Legal Services Corporation, the American Association of Law Schools, and the National Legal Aid and Defender Association. The desirability of minority membership should be considered in making appointments. If Congress adopts a statute on the subject, precatory language on the need for broadened membership on the committees would suffice.

Neither Congress nor the President should be represented on the Standing or advisory committees. Even the presence of congressional observers may give senior congressional members who designate them a disproportionate influence in rule-making and tend to co-opt Congress so that an independent judgment on the rules may not be possible.

7. The Standing Committee should widely publicize the proposals of its advisory committees and hold public hearings before recommending adoption to the Judicial Conference. The Standing Committee should not hesitate to request factual studies from such groups as the United States Judicial Center, the American Bar Foundation, the American Law Institute, law schools, and others where the Standing Committee's or an advisory committee's judgment has been seriously questioned. Thorough airing of the issues before adoption may reduce congressional desire to review the details of proposed rules.

8. The original drafts of the advisory committees should, as they have in the past, be supported by extensive notes. Where the Standing Committee or the Judicial Conference makes changes they should be explained in accompanying notes.[522]

VI:B. Suggested Changes in Local Rule-Making and Guideline-Making Process and in Rule-Making by Individual Judges

1. No local rule for an appellate or trial court should be adopted without publishing the proposal in advance

and providing for a public hearing on notice. Here, as in the case of national rules, publicity is an "effort to obtain democratization of the rule-making process without destroying its flexibility by imposing procedural requirements that are too onerous."[523] Mere publication will not be enough; affirmative efforts to engage the bar, bench, and law schools in the work will be needed. Thus, each court should be encouraged to utilize a pattern of advisory committees for rule-making that would call on cooperating representatives of the public, including lay persons. There is little danger that good proposals will be talked and studied to death without regard to their merits.

2. To preserve national uniformity and control excessive or unwise local rule-making, no local rule, other than one of the Supreme Court, should be effective, until it has been reported to the Standing Committee on National Rules of Court Practice and Procedure and the Standing Committee has approved it. If the Standing Committee fails to approve within six months, or if it rejects a rule, the United States Judicial Conference should have the right of approval. To meet emergency situations a court should have the power to adopt a local rule for no more than one year.

3. Guidelines or their equivalent adopted for a court by itself or by a committee of a court or by an appellate court, judicial council, circuit, judicial conference, or by the United States Judicial Conference should be published before they become effective. Upon objection by any person, a public hearing should be held.

4. Individual judges should eliminate, so far as possible, individual rules affecting their own practice that

diverge from those of other judges on their court. Local courtwide rules are preferable.

5. All local rules, guidelines, or judge's rules should be made available in a readily usable and up-to-date form to the bench, bar, and public.

VI:C. Availability of All Materials to Public

All documents considered in connection with any rule or guideline adopted by the United States Judicial Conference or by any court should be made available to the press or any member of the public on simple demand. Public hearings should be recorded and a transcript made similarly available. Wherever possible, reasons for the rules should be put in writing following the analogous practice of Congress in preparing committee reports to support legislation and the practice of the present advisory committees whose notes have been extremely valuable to the bench and bar. These materials will assist courts in interpreting the rules,[524] and will protect against arbitrary conduct or the suspicion of arbitrary conduct.[525]

VI:D. Initiating the Changes in Rule-Making Process

Recommendations for changes in the rule-making process could come with propriety, as they have in the past, from any one of the branches of government. Since the Judicial Conference of the United States is already under the duty of studying the "operation and effect" of rules[526] it would seem desirable to allow the Conference and its committees a reasonable time to suggest whether and what kind of changes in rule-making procedures are desirable. Congress can then act on these recommendations for change with the assistance of the executive branch. Should the courts fail to act within a reasonable time, Congress or the executive should then take the initiative.

There is much that is admirable in the present system. It has worked well. There is no guarantee that any modified system will work better. But given the risks and the possible gains, my own judgment is that a change is now desirable. Since we are not dealing with demonstrable mathematical formulas but in judgments based upon personal experience and history, I recognize that others who have my respect will differ with me. If they do, I hope that they will speak out so that the matter can be thoroughly debated.

NOTES

1. See, *e.g.*, The Compact Edition of the Oxford English Dictionary (1971) ("Rule ... 4. *Law* ... b. A formal order of regulation governing the procedure or decisions of a court of law.... Also called a (standing) *rule of court.*") (emphasis in original); Black's Law Dictionary (1957) ("Rule.... General Rules. General or standing orders of a court, in relation to practice, etc." "Rules of Court. The rules for regulating the practice of the different courts, which the judges are empowered to frame and put in force as occasion may require."); 2 Bouvier's Law Dictionary (1914) ("Rule of Court.... Rules of court are either general or special; the former are the laws by which the practice of the court is governed; the latter are special orders made in particular cases."); Federal Rules of Civil Procedure; New York Civil Practice Law and Rules.

2. Professor Hazard, Jr., uses the term "rule-making" to refer to both formally promulgated rules and significant reformulation of decisional law in litigated cases: "rule-making includes ... the procedures used by courts and agencies performing adjudicative functions in adopting rules of procedure and rules governing their own internal administration;—the procedures used by appellate courts when they contemplate significant reformulation of decisional law." Hazard, *Representation in Rule-making,* in Law and the American Future 85, 87 (M.L. Schwartz ed. 1976). It is only in the former sense that the term is used in this discussion. *Cf.* B. Schwartz & H.W.R. Wade, Legal Control of Government 84ff. (1972) (rule-making by general regulations of administrative bodies as delegated legislation).

3. For various bibliographies on the subject and summaries of rule-making in United States jurisdictions, see, *e.g.*, F.J. Klein, Judicial Administration and the Legal Profession, A Bibliography 290 et seq. (1963) (I have had the advantage of the manuscript for the 1976 edition of this invaluable book); C. Sherr, Bibliography—Rule-Making Power of the Courts, 1928-1955 (1955) (unpublished bibliography on file at the Columbia Law School Library); American Judicature Society, Uses of the Judicial Rule-Making Power (1974) (mimeograph); J.A. Parness and C.A.

Korbakes, A Study of the Procedural Rule-Making Power in the United States 68-76 (August, 1973) (mimeograph); American Judicature Society, The Judicial Rule-Making Power in State Court Systems (October, 1967) (mimeograph); Ashman, Measuring the Judicial Rule-Making Power, 59 Judicature 215 (1975) (summarizes the excellent studies of the American Judicature Society); *Study of Rule-Making Power*, in New York Advisory Committee on Practice & Procedure, Third Preliminary Report 825 ff. (Leg. Doc. No. 17, 1959) (Weinstein, Reporter); American Bar Association, Standards Relating to Court Organization 76 (1974); Blau and Clark, *Sources of Rules of State Courts*, 66 Law Library Journal 37 (1973); Annots.: 110 A.L.R. 22 (1973); 158 A.L.R. 705 (1945).

4. *Compare* Winberry v. Salisbury, 5 N.J. 240, 74 A.2d 406, *cert. denied*, 340 U.S. 877, 71 S.Ct. 123 (1950), with N.J.S.A. 2A:84A-39.1-.6 (Supp. 1975) (State Rules of Court Review Commission).

5. See N.Y.C.P.L.R. § 102 (McKinney 1972); N.Y. Judiciary Law § 229(3) (McKinney 1968).

6. Civil and general local rules are collected in loose leaf form in the Federal Rules Service. Federal Local Court Rules (H. Fischer and J. Willis eds. 1972). There is no national collection of criminal rules.

7. 28 U.S.C.A., United States Courts of Appeals Rules (1969).

8. *See, e.g.*, rules for various New York courts collected in M. Bender, New York 1975-76 Civil Practice Annual (1975).

9. See *Hearings on Proposed Rules of Evidence Before the Special Subcomm. on Reform of Federal Criminal Laws, House Comm. on the Judiciary*, 93d Cong., 1st Sess., ser. 2, at 145 (1973) (testimony of Justice Arthur J. Goldberg: ". . . each Justice studies those rules. He is not given the benefit of any adversary report. . . . In the conference of the Court, a vote is taken as to whether the rule shall be submitted to Congress.").

10. Miranda v. Arizona, 384 U.S. 436, 86 S.Ct. 1602, 16 L.Ed.2d 694 (1966); *cf.* Vorenberg, *A.L.I. Approves Model Code of Pre-Arraignment Procedure*, 61 A.B.A.J. 1212, 1213 (1975).

11. But *cf.* Address by Judge Lumbard, "Criminal Justice and the Rule Making Power," to Conference of Chief Justices in Honolulu, August 3, 1967.

The criticism of *Miranda* is on the ground that the matter should have been treated by rule-making, particularly since the American Law Institute was considering the matter as part of its work on prearraignment procedures.

12. *See* Mildner v. Gulotta, et al., 405 F.Supp. 182, 201 (E.D.N.Y. 1975), *aff'd* 425 U.S. 901, 96 Sup. Ct. 1489 (1976) (dissent by Weinstein, J., based on minimum standards of right to be heard and to reasoned opinion in court cases).

13. See Monaghan, *The Supreme Court 1974 Term, Forward: Constitutional Common Law,* 89 Harv. L. Rev. 1 (1975).

14. U.S. Const. amend. I: "The right of the people . . . to petition the Government for a redress of grievances."

15. Compare this route with that of requiring "standing" in courts. Mr. Justice Powell, concurring in United States v. Richardson, 418 U.S. 166, 188-89, 94 S.Ct. 2940, 2952 (1974) noted:

[T] he argument that the Court should allow unrestricted taxpayer or citizen standing underestimates the ability of the representative branches of the Federal Government to respond to the citizen pressure that has been responsible in large measure for the current drift toward expanded standing. Indeed, taxpayer or citizen advocacy, given its potentially broad base, is precisely the type of leverage that in a democracy ought to be employed against the branches that were intended to be responsive to public attitudes about the appropriate operation of government. "We must as judges recall that, as Mr. Justice Holmes wisely observed, the other branches of the Government 'are ultimate guardians of the liberties and welfare of the people in quite as great a degree as the courts.' Missouri, Kansas & Texas R. Co. v. May, 194 U.S. 267, 270." Flast v. Cohen, 392 U.S., at 131 (Mr. Justice Harlan, dissenting).

Unrestrained standing in federal taxpayer or citizen suits would create a remarkably illogical system of judicial supervision of the coordinate branches of the Federal Government.

16. M. Rosenberg & J.B. Weinstein, Elements of Civil Procedure (1st ed. 1962).

17. *Cf.* Weinstein, *Routine Bifurcation of Jury Negligence Trials: An Example of the Questionable Use of Rule-Making Power,* 14 Vand. L. Rev. 831 (1961).

18. See, *e.g., Study of Rule-Making Power* in New York Advisory Committee on Practice and Procedure, Third Preliminary Report 825 ff. (Leg. Doc. No. 17, 1959) (Weinstein, Reporter).

19. Part of the story is told in the *Preface* to 1 J.B. Weinstein, H. Korn & A. Miller, New York Civil Practice (1963). *See also, e.g.,* Weinstein, *Proposed Revision of New York Civil Practice,* 60 Colum. L. Rev. 60 (1960); Weinstein, *Responsibility for Civil Practice Revision,* 145 N.Y.L.J. (1961).

20. Some aspects of the history of the committee's work are referred to in the *Preface* to 1 J.B. Weinstein & M. Berger, Weinstein's Evidence (1975).

21. Weinstein, *The Uniformity-Conformity Dilemma Facing Draftsmen of Federal Rules of Evidence,* 69 Colum. L. Rev. 353 (1969). *Cf.* Weinstein, *Some Difficulties in Devising Rules for Determining Truth in Judicial Trials,* 66 Colum. L. Rev. 223 (1966).

22. See *e.g.,* J. B. Weinstein & M. Berger, Weinstein's Evidence, *Preface* viii (1975); 3 *Id.* ¶ 609[01]; 2 *Id.* ¶ 509[01].

23. Hungate, *Changes in the Federal Rules of Criminal Procedure,* 61 A.B.J. 1203, 1207 (1975).

24. See, *e.g.,* Weinstein, *Proper and Improper Interactions Between Bench and Law School,* 50 St. John's L. Rev. 441 (1976); Weinstein, *Questionable Proposals to Make Admission to the Federal Bar More Difficult,* ALI-ABA CLE Review, Dec. 5, 12, 19 (1975); Amendment to Rule 25.2 of the General Rules for the Southern and Eastern Districts of New York, adopted September 22, 1975, fixing amounts to be posted as collateral for violation of federal wildlife protection laws and regulations, amendment with no notice to the public (Weinstein, J. dissenting).

25. Marbury v. Madison, 5 U.S. (1 Cranch) 87, 2 L.Ed. 60 (1803). The increasing tendency of federal courts not to intervene needs to be noted. *Cf.* Mitchum v. Foster, 407 U.S. 225, 92 S.Ct. 2151 (1972) (Chief Justice concurring in reliance on Younger v. Harris, 401 U.S. 37, 91 S.Ct. 746, 27 L.Ed.2d 669 (1971)).

26. *Cf.* Ehrlich, *Legal Pollution, Increasingly often, there ought "not" to be a law,* N.Y. Times Magazine, Feb. 8, 1976, at 17.
The burdens of all this expanded court intervention and growth of litigation on the middle class can not be ignored. *Cf.* Weinstein,

Notes

The Delivery of Legal Services, N.Y.L.J., at 1, May 1, 1974; Weinstein, *All People are Entitled to Lawyers in Civil Matters,* N.Y.L.J., at 1, April 1, 2, 1976.

27. This is not to say that there were no departures from this doctrine, as we are reminded by such historical favorites as Marbury v. Madison, 5 U.S. (1 Cranch) 137, 2 L.Ed. 60 (1803); Dred Scott v. Sanford, 60 U.S. (19 How.) 393, 15 L.Ed. 691 (1857); the Slaughterhouse cases, 83 U.S. (16 Wall.) 36, 21 L.Ed. 394 (1873); and Plessy v. Ferguson, 163 U.S. 537, 16 S.Ct. 138, 41 L.Ed. 256 (1896).

28. Chief Justice Burger, "The Condition of the Judiciary," 1975 Year-end Report, January 3, 1976: "The tendency of Americans to try to resolve every sort of problem in the courts continues. Overwhelmed by increased demands for regulatory legislation, for broadened governmental programs of all kinds, Congress enacts legislation much of which reaches the courts for resolution."

29. 42 U.S.C. § 2000e (1970).

30. See Albemarle v. Moody, 422 U.S. 405, 95 S.Ct. 2362 (1975); Griggs v. Duke Power Co., 401 U.S. 424 (1971); E.E.O.C. Guidelines, 29 C.F.R. § 1607 (1974).

31. United States Department of Agriculture v. Murry, 413 U.S. 508, 519, 93 S.Ct. 2832, 2838, 37 L.Ed.2d 767 (1973) (Marshall, J., concurring). *See also, e.g.,* S.A. Scheingold, The Politics of Rights 119 (1974) ("particularization seems to be consistent with the preference of most judges. . . . The consequence is to break compliance down into a series of one-on-one confrontations that play into the hands of those who oppose the rules [in their case-law sense] promulgated by the judges.").

32. *See, e.g.,* Tribe, *Structured Due Process,* 10 Harv. Civ. Rights–Civ. Lib. L. Rev. 269 (1975); Note, *Irrebuttable Presumptions: An Illusory Analysis,* 27 Stan. L. Rev. 449 (1975); Note, *Irrebuttable Presumptions as an Alternative to Strict Scrutiny: From Rodriguez to La Fleur,* 62 Geo. L. J. 1173 (1974).

33. Mathews v. Eldridge, 424 U.S. 319, 344 (1976).

34. Crawford v. Cushman, 531 F.2d 1114, 1125 (2d Cir. 1976). But see Ehrlich, *Legal Pollution, Increasingly often, there*

ought "not" to be a law, N.Y. Times Magazine, Feb. 8, 1976, at 17.

35. Class actions, however, have obviously made some of the appellate courts nervous. *Cf.* Wallace v. Kern, 499 F.2d 1345 (2d Cir. 1974) (wholesale relief for hundreds of prisoners held for excessive periods awaiting trial impermissible). See, *e.g.,* Weinstein, *Some Reflections on the "Abusiveness" of Class Actions,* 58 F.R.D. 299 (1973). See Note, *[New York] Legislature Adopts Liberal Class Action Statute,* 50 St. John's L. Rev. 189 (1975).

36. See 28 U.S.C. § 1407 (1970). A brief history of the Judicial Panel on Multidistrict Litigation is set forth in the *Foreword* to the Manual for Complex and Multidistrict Litigation, xi-xii (West 1970) prepared by a committee of federal judges in consultation with professors and members of the bar.

37. See, *e.g.,* M. Rosenberg, J.B. Weinstein, H. Smit, H. Korn, Elements of Civil Procedure, ch. 15, § 4 (1976).

38. See, *e.g.,* on standing: United States v. Students Challenging Regulatory Agency Procedures, 412 U.S. 699, 93 S.Ct. 2405 (1974); Sierra Club v. Morton, 405 U.S. 727, 92 S.Ct. 1261 (1972); Flast v. Cohen, 392 U.S. 83, 88 S.Ct. 1942 (1968). *Cf.* Hawaii v. Standard Oil Co. of California, 405 U.S. 251, 92 S.Ct. 885 (1972); the Clean Air Act, 42 U.S.C. § 1857h-2(a) (1970); Jaffe, *Standing Again,* 84 Harv. L. Rev. 633 (1971); Davis, *The Liberalized Law of Standing,* 37 U. Chi. L. Rev. 450 (1970).

Limitation of the "political issue" doctrine has closed off, to some extent, an escape from federal court intervention. See, *e.g.,* Baker v. Carr, 369 U.S. 186, 82 S.Ct. 691, 7 L.Ed.2d 663 (1962).

39. *See, e.g.,* Rosenbluth v. Finkelstein, 300 N.Y. 402, 404, 91 N.E.2d 581 (1950); Annot. 132 A.L.R. 1185 (1941).

40. Buckley v. Valego, 424 U.S. 1, 113-18, 96 S.Ct. 612, 680 (1976).

41. *See, e.g.,* Robinson v. Cahill, 67 N.J. 333, 339 A. 2d 193 (1975); Hicks v. New Mexico, 88 N.M. 588, 544 P.2d 1153 (1976) (abolition of doctrine of immunity only to future cases). See also L. Luskey, By What Right? 76-79 (1975).

42. American Law Institute, Study of the Division of Jurisdiction Between State and Federal Courts 292-96 (1969); Note, *Scope of Certification,* 29 Rutgers L. Rev. 1155 (1976).

43. Milliken v. Green, 389 Mich. 1, 203 N.W.2d 457 (1972), *vacated* as improvident advisory opinion, 390 Mich. 389, 212 N.W.2d 711 (1973). See notes 121, 162, 165, 175, *infra.*

44. 367 U.S. 643, 81 S.Ct. 1684, 6 L.Ed.2d 1081 (1961).

45. Monaghan, *The Supreme Court 1974 Term, Forward: Constitutional Common Law,* 89 Harv. L. Rev. 1, 2 (1975).

46. J. Greenberg, Litigation for Social Change: Methods, Limits and Role in Democracy (1973).

47. See *e.g.*, Annual State of Judiciary Message of Chief Justice Burger to American Bar Association, crediting much of recent improvement to courts rather than Congress, N.Y. Times, Feb. 16, 1976, at 1, col. 1.

48. Sunderland, *Implementing the Rule-Making Power,* 25 N.Y.U.L. Rev. 27, 29 (1950).

49. See, *e.g.*, J.A. Parness and C.A. Korbakes, A Study of the Procedural Rule-making Power in the United States, August, 1973 (mimeograph) (setting forth an analysis of the practice in each of the states).

50. *Id.* at 4-12 (discussion of the variety of "model" judicial articles and provisions that have varied over the years).

51. American Bar Association Commission on Standards of Judicial Administration, Standards Relating to Court Organization, 63 (Tentative Draft, 1973). The Standards Relating to Court Organization, adopted by the ABA House of Delegates in February, 1974, was different in form but not substance. American Bar Association, Standards Relating to Court Organization §§ 1.30, 1.31, pp. 71-72 (1974).

52. Calif. Const. art. VI, § 1a; A.T. Vanderbilt, Minimum Standards of Judicial Administration 130 (1949).

53. N.Y. Judiciary Law § 229 (McKinney 1968).

54. J.A. Parness and C.A. Korbakes, A Study of the Procedural Rule-Making Power in the United States 18 (August, 1973) (mimeograph).

55. Sunderland, *Implementing the Rule-Making Power,* 25 N.Y.U.L. Rev. 27, 41 (1950).

56. The extent of courts' powers to establish rules concerning courtroom procedures and standards outside of the focus of cases and controversies has varied extensively. The Romans, particularly in criminal law, unified executive and judicial functions in executive officials. Thus a notion of rule-making as a function of an independent judiciary did not exist. F. Abbott, A History and Description of Roman Political Institutions 284-85, 346-49, 363-65, 367-68 (1901). Current research by the author in Israel indicates that the judges, the Knesset (parliament), organs of the Ministry of Justice, the law schools, and the bar have important roles in rule-making. See J. Weinstein, Court Procedures in Israel: Rule Making, N.Y.L.V. June 1977.

57. See generally R. Walker & M. Walker, The English Legal System 3-13 (2d ed. 1970).

58. 1 J. Goebel, Jr., History of the Supreme Court of the United States 23 (1971).

59. 1 Montesquieu, Spirit of the Laws, Books 1 and 2 (Dublin ed. 1971).

60. Case of Prohibitions del Roy, 12 Coke's Rep. 63 (1607) (Coke, C.J.). See also, *e.g.*, *In Re* The Bishop of Natal, 3 Moo. Privy Council (n.s.) 115 (1864) (Crown no longer has a general power to create new courts).

61. Henry St. John Viscount Bolingbroke, A Dissertation upon Portier, Letter X at 108, Letter XII at 138 (3d ed. 1735).

62. *Id.*, Letter XII at 138.

63. 8 Coke Rep. 107 (1610).

64. 8 Coke Rep. 107, 118 (1610). See generally 1 J. Goebel, Jr., History of the Supreme Court of the United States 92-95 (1971); Boudin, *Lord Coke and the American Doctrine of Judicial Power*, 6 N.Y.U.L. Rev. 223 (1929); Plucknett, *Bonham's Case and Judicial Review*, 40 Harv. L. Rev. 30 (1926); Corwin, *The "Higher Law" Background of American Constitutional Law*, 42 Harv. L. Rev. 365 (1928).

65. 1 Blackstone, Commentaries 91 (1830 ed.).

66. See generally, R. Walker & M. Walker, The English Legal System 17-26 (2d ed., 1970).

67. *Id.* at 60.

68. *Id.* at 54-62.

69. *Id.* at 26.

70. Judicature Act, 1875 (§ 17); Appellate Jurisdiction Act, 1876 (§ 17); Judicature Act, 1881 (§ 19); Judicature Act, 1894 (§ 4); Rule Committee Act, 1909. See S. Rosenbaum, The Rule-Making Authority in the English Supreme Court 21, n.1 (1917). Both Houses of Parliament reserved the right to veto (§ 25 of the Judicature Act, 1875) but neither seems to have exercised that right. S. Rosenbaum, The Rule-Making Authority in the English Supreme Court 26, n.9 (1917).

71. S. Rosenbaum, The Rule-Making Authority in the English Supreme Court 264-67 (1917).

72. See Judicature Act of 1925, § 99.

73. See County Courts Act of 1959, § 102.

74. See Matrimonial Causes Act of 1973, § 50.

75. Section 99(1) of the Judicature Act of 1925 empowers the Supreme Court Rule Committee to make rules for the following purposes:

(a) For regulating and prescribing the procedure (including the method of pleading) and the practice to be followed in the Court of Appeal and the High Court respectively in all causes and matters whatsoever in or with respect to which those courts respectively have for the time being jurisdiction (including the procedure and practice to be followed in the offices of the Supreme Court and in district registries), and any matters incidental to or relating to any such procedure or practice, including (but without prejudice to the generality of the foregoing provision) the manner in which, and the time within which, any applications which under this or any other Act are to be made to the Court of Appeal or to the High Court shall be made:

(b) For regulating and prescribing the procedure on appeals from any court or person to the Court of Appeal or the High Court, and the procedure in connection with the transfer of proceedings from any inferior court to the High Court or from the High Court to an inferior court:

(c) For regulating the sittings of the Court of Appeal and the High Court, of the divisional courts of the High Court, and of the judges of the High Court whether sitting in court or in chambers:

(d) For prescribing what part of the business which may be transacted and of the jurisdiction which may be exercised by judges of the High Court in chambers may be transacted or exercised by masters of the Supreme Court, registrars of the Probate Division, or other officers of the Supreme Court:

(e) For regulating any matters relating to the costs of proceedings in the Court of Appeal or the High Court:

(f) For regulating and prescribing the procedure and practice to be followed in the Court of Appeal or the High Court in cases in which the procedure or practice is regulated by enactments in force immediately before the commencement of this Act or by any provisions of this Act re-enacting any such enactments (including so much of any of the Acts set out in the First Schedule of this Act as is specified in the third column of that Schedule):

(g) For repealing any enactments which relate to matters with respect to which rules are made under this section:

(h) For prescribing in what cases trials in the High Court are to be with a jury and in what cases they are to be without a jury:

(i) For regulating the means by which particular facts may be proved, and the mode in which evidence thereof may be given, in any proceedings or on any application in connection with or at any stage of any proceedings:

(j) For regulating or making provision with respect to any other matters which are regulated or with respect to which provision was made by the rules of the Supreme Court in force on the thirtieth day of September, nineteen hundred and twenty-five, or by any rules or regulations so in force with respect to practice and procedure in matrimonial causes and matters or with respect to applications and proceedings relating to legitimacy declarations.

76. Jacob, Memorandum on the Machinery of the Rule Committee of the Supreme Court (unpublished draft, 1970) ¶ 7

(hereinafter, Jacob memorandum). Reprinted by kind permission of Senior Master Jacob.

77. See §§ 102(1)-(3) of the County Court Act of 1959 and § 50(1) of the Matrimonial Causes Act of 1973.

78. See, *e.g.*, Administration of Justice Act 1969, §§ 20 and 21, enabling powers to make rules of court relating to "orders for interim payments" and "to inspection etc. of property before commencement of action," and to the rules of evidence, *e.g.*, Evidence Act 1938, § 5, and Civil Evidence Act 1968, § 8.

79. R. Walker & M. Walker, The English Legal System, 61 (2d ed. 1970).

80. *Id.* at 223.

81. *Id.* at 61.

82. Interview with R.C.L. Gregory, legal advisor to the Lord Chancellor, secretary of County Court and Matrimonial Causes Rule committees by Keith Secular, of the New York Bar, Jan. 15, 1976 (hereinafter Gregory interview).

83. *Id.*

84. See, *e.g.*, Law Reform Committee, Thirteenth Report (Cmnd. 2964, 1966); Evidence Act of 1968; J.M. Maguire, J.B. Weinstein, J.M. Chadbourn & J.H. Mansfield, Cases & Materials on Evidence, 808-13 (6th ed. 1973). The English Evidence Act of 1938, with some modifications, has been widely adopted in former colonies. See, *e.g.*, E.J. Edwards, Cases of Evidence in Australia 601 (1968).

85. See Cross, *An Attempt to Update the Law of Evidence*, 9 Israeli L. Rev. 1, 2 (1974); R. Walker & M. Walker, The English Legal System 97-98 (1st ed. 1967) (Law Commissions Act of 1965); Criminal Law Revision Committee, Eleventh Report, Evidence (Comnd. 4991, 1972).

86. Jacob memorandum ¶ 2(a).

87. County Court Act of 1959, § 102(8); Matrimonial Causes Act of 1973, § 50(1).

88. Jacob memorandum ¶ 1. See Judicature Act of 1925, § 99(4).

89. The County Court Rule Committee consists of five judges of County Courts, two barristers, two solicitors, and two registrars. County Court Act of 1959, § 102(6). The Matrimonial Causes Rule Committee consists of The Lord Chancellor, the president of the Family Division, a judge of that division, two registrars, two circuit judges, two barristers, and two solicitors. Matrimonial Causes Act of 1973, § 50(1).

90. Jacob memorandum ¶ 3.

91. Gregory interview.

92. Jacob memorandum ¶ 16.

93. Jacob memorandum ¶ 11.

94. See, *e.g.*, Order 22 rule 2 referred to in A. Martin French v. Kingswood Hill Limited, [1960] 1 Q.B. 96, discussed in Jacob memorandum ¶ 13.

95. *Id.*

96. *Id.*

97. Gregory interview.

98. Jacob memorandum ¶ 16.

99. *Id.* ¶ 17.

100. *Id.* ¶ 18.

101. Gregory interview.

102. Jacob memorandum ¶ 20; Gregory interview.

103. *Id.*

104. Gregory interview.

105. Jacob memorandum ¶ 20.

106. *Id.* ¶ 5.

107. *Id.* ¶ 8.

108. *Id.*

109. Gregory interview.

110. Jacob memorandum ¶ 7. See Judicature Act of 1925, County Court Act of 1959, § 102(9), Matrimonial Causes Act of 1973, § 50(4).

111. See, *In Re* Grosvenor Hotel, London (No. 2) [1965] 1 Ch. 1210 (1965), [1964] 3 All E.R. 354; Ward v. James, [1966] 1 Q.B. 273, [1965] 1 All E.R. 563; *Cf.,* Final Report of the Committee on Supreme Court Practice and Procedure 84-86 (presented to Parliament in 1953).

112. Jacob memorandum ¶ 8, citing the example of Lord Denning, who was a member of the relevant rule committee, holding that Order 20, rule 5, which empowers the Court to allow amendments after the expiration of the current period of limitation in specified cases is *intra vires* (Mitchell v. Harris Engineering Company Limited, [1967] 2 Q.D. 703) but that the former Order 24 rule 15, insofar as it purported to alter the rules relating to Crown privilege was *ultra vires* (*re* Grosvenor Hotel, London (No. 2), [1965] 1 Ch. 1210).

113. Jacob memorandum ¶ 21.

114. S. Rosenbaum, The Rule-Making Authority in the English Supreme Court 2 (1917).

115. 1 J. Goebel, Jr., History of the Supreme Court of the United States 103-4 (1971).

116. *Id.* at 98, n.9.

117. See L. Baker, John Marshall, A Life in Law 91 (1974).

118. 4 P.L. Ford, ed., The Works of Thomas Jefferson, "Notes on the State of Virginia" 21 (Fed. ed. 1904-5).

119. See, 1 J. Goebel, Jr., History of the Supreme Court of the United States 99 n.14 (1971).

120. Mass. Const., art. 3, ch. 3 (1780).

121. H. Hart and H. Wechsler, The Federal Courts and the Federal System 69 (2d ed. P. Bator, P. Mishkin, D. Shapiro & H. Wechsler 1973). See generally, Field, *The Advisory Opinion—an Analysis,* 24 Ind. L.J. 203 (1949); Stevens, *Advisory Opinions—Present Status and an Evaluation,* 34 Wash. L.J. 1 (1959); Edsall, *The Advisory Opinion in North Carolina,* 27 N.C.L. Rev. 297 (1947); Sands, *Government by Judiciary—Advisory Opinions in Alabama,* 4 Ala. L. Rev. 1 (1951); Hageman, *The Advisory Opinion in South Dakota* 16 S.D.L. Rev. 291 (1971); In the Matter of the Application of the Senate, 10 Minn. 78 (1865) (holding the statute unconstitutional); *In Re* Opinions of the

167

Justices, 209 Ala. 593, 96 So. 487 (1923) (upholding advisory opinion statute).

122. Nelson, *The Reform of Common Law Pleading in Massachusetts 1760-1830: Adjudication as a Prelude to Legislation*, 122 Pa. L. Rev. 97 (1973).

123. 1 J. Goebel, Jr., History of the Supreme Court of the United States, 204 (1971).

124. C.C. Tansill, ed., Documents Illustrative of the Formation of the Union of the American States, House Rep. Doc. No. 398, 69th Cong., 1st Sess. 955 (1927).

125. I The Records of the Federal Convention of 1787, 97 (M. Farrand ed. 1937).

126. *Id.* II at 22.

127. 1 J. Goebel, Jr., History of the Supreme Court of the United States, 241 (1971).

128. See generally on the issue of judicial review as raised at the Philadelphia Convention, E. Corwin, The Doctrine of Judicial Review 10-27 (1914); C. Beard, The Supreme Court and the Constitution 15-67 (1912); H. Davis, The Judicial Veto (1914); G. Dietze, The Federalist, A Classic on Federalism and Free Government 129, 171-75, 277-81 (1960); R.H. Jackson, The Struggle for Judicial Supremacy 3-17 (1940).

129. E. Corwin, The Doctrine of Judicial Review 11-12 (1913) (footnotes omitted).

130. Hamilton, The Federalist, No. 78, 420 (1818 ed.).

131. *Id.*

132. *Id.* (Emphasis in original.) These provisions for life appointment, for tenure under good behavior, and a preclusion of salary reductions (see Federalist No. 79) are crucial in preserving the judiciary as an independent and separate arm for upholding justice.

133. *Id.*

134. *Id.* at 421.

135. *Id.* at 422.

Notes

136. J.T. Main, The Antifederalists: Critics of the Constitution, 1781-1788, 158 (1961).

137. 1 J. Goebel, Jr., History of the Supreme Court of the United States 281 (1971).

138. See R.A. Rutland, George Mason, Reluctant Statesman (1961).

139. *Id.* at 379, 384-85.

140. *Id.* at 385.

141. III The Debates in the Several State Conventions on the Adoption of the Federal Constitution, as Recommended by the General Convention at Philadelphia in 1787, 553 (J. Elliot ed. 1881).

142. Although judicial review was mentioned in the Pennsylvania, New York, North Carolina, and Massachusetts conventions, the only full debate was at the Virginia Convention. See, G. Dietze, The Federalist, A Classic on Federalism and Free Government 172 n.2 (1960).

143. The letter read as follows:

Philadelphia, July 18, 1793.

Gentlemen:

The war which has taken place among the powers of Europe produces frequent transactions within our ports and limits, on which questions arise of considerable difficulty, and of greater importance to the peace of the United States. These questions depend for their solution on the construction of our treaties, on the laws of nature and nations, and on the laws of the land, and are often presented under circumstances *which do not give a cognizance of them to the tribunals of the country.* Yet their decision is so little analogous to the ordinary functions of the executive, as to occasion much embarrassment and difficulty to them. The President therefore would be much relieved if he found himself free to refer questions of this description to the opinions of the judges of the Supreme Court of the United States, whose knowledge of the subject would secure us against errors dangerous to the peace of the United States, and their authority insure the respect of all parties. He has therefore asked the attendance of such of the judges as could be collected in time for the occasion, to know, in the first place, their opinion, whether the public may, with propriety, be availed of their *advice on these questions*? And if they may, to present, for their advice, the abstract questions which have already occurred, or may soon occur, from which they will themselves strike out such as any circumstances might, in their opinion, forbid them to pronounce on. I have the honour to be with sentiments of the most perfect respect, gentlemen,

Your most obedient and humble servant,

Thos. Jefferson.

3 Johnston, Correspondence and Public Papers of John Jay 486 (1891) (*reprinted in* H. Hart & H. Wechsler, The Federal Courts and the Federal System 64 (2d ed. P. Bator, P. Mishkin, D. Shapiro & H. Wechsler 1973)).

Earlier, the Chief Justice had rejected overtures for support from Jefferson's political foe, Secretary of the Treasury Hamilton. See Dilliard, *John Jay*, in 1 The Justices of the United States Supreme Court 13-14 (L. Friedman & F. Israel eds. 1969).

144. 10 Sparks, Writings of Washington 542-45 (1836) (*reprinted in* Hart and Wechsler, *id.* at 64-65).

145. The letter to President Washington reads:

Sir:

We have considered the previous question stated in a letter written by your direction to us by the Secretary of State on the 18th of last month, [regarding] the lines of separation drawn by the Constitution between the three departments of the government. These being in certain respects checks upon each other, and our being judges of a court in the last resort, are considerations which afford strong arguments against the propriety of our extrajudicially deciding the questions alluded to, especially as the power given by the Constitution to the President, of calling on the heads of departments for opinions, seems to have been *purposely* as well as expressly united to the *executive* departments.

We exceedingly regret every event that may cause embarrassment to your administration, but we derive consolation from the reflection that your judgment will discern what is right, and that your usual prudence, decision, and firmness will surmount every obstacle to the preservation of the rights, peace, and dignity of the United States.

3 Johnston, Correspondence and Public Papers of John Jay 488 (1891) (*reprinted in* H. Hart and H. Wechsler, *id.* at 65-66). Jay had previously served as a principal draftsman of the New York Constitution of 1777, which placed veto power over legislation in a Council of Revision (analogous to the English Privy Council) composed of the governor, the chancellor, and New York's Supreme Court justices. G. Pellew, John Jay 81-82 (J. Morse ed. 1890). Later, as Chief Justice of New York during the Revolution, Jay served as a member of the Council of Revision. *Id.* at 92. Despite his earlier design of and participation in an agency that blurred the distinction between the three branches, Jay was adamant in the letter to Washington that the Federal Constitution required a strict separation.

146. See 3 K. Davis, Administrative Law Treatise 127-28 (1958).

147. See 1 J. Goebel, Jr., History of the Supreme Court of the United States 560 (1971).

148. Act of Mar. 23, 1792, ch. 11 § 2, 1 Stat. 243.

149. Statement of C.C.N.Y., quoted in Hayburn's Case, 2 U.S. (2 Dall.) 355, 356 n.a (1792) (Jay and Cushing, Circuit Justices, Duane, D.J.).

150. Letter of C.C.Pa. to the President, quoted in Hayburn's Case, 2 U.S. (2 Dall.) 355, 357 (1792) (Wilson and Blair, Circuit Justices, Peters, D.J.).

151. 2 U.S. (2 Dall.) 355 (1792).

152. Act of Feb. 28, 1793, ch. 17, 1 Stat. 324. See generally 1 J. Goebel, Jr., History of the Supreme Court of the United States 560-64 (1971).

153. Letter of George Washington to the Chief Justice and Associate Justices of the Supreme Court, April 3, 1790 (*reprinted in* 1 J. Goebel, Jr., History of the Supreme Court of the United States 555 (1971)).

154. See 2 Story, Commentaries on the Constitution § 1579 n.1 (5th ed. Bigelow 1891).

155. 1 J. Goebel, Jr., History of the Supreme Court of the United States 554-69 (1971).

156. Stuart v. Laird, 5 U.S. (1 Cranch) 186, 191 (1803).

157. 1 Warren, The Supreme Court in United States History 596-97 (1937 ed.); C.E. Hughes, The Supreme Court of the United States 30-31 (1928).

158. See Tyler, Memoir of Roger B. Taney 433-34 (1872). See the discussion in O'Malley v. Woodrough, 307 U.S. 277, 287-89, 75 S.Ct. 838, 842-43 (1939).

159. See Evans v. Gore, 253 U.S. 245, 40 S.Ct. 550 (1920) (tax held invalid); O'Malley v. Woodrough, 307 U.S. 277, 59 S.Ct. 838 (1939) (overruled *Evans*.). *Cf.* the suit by some federal judges to require compensation to offset inflation. N.Y.L.J., Feb. 13, 1976, at 1, col. 2.

160. C.E. Hughes, The Supreme Court of the United States 31 (1928).

161. 219 U.S. 346, 31 S.Ct. 250 (1911).

162. See also Liberty-Warehouse Co. v. Grannis, 273 U.S. 70, 47 S.Ct. 282 (1924); United States v. Fruehauf, 365 U.S. 146, 157 (1961), and cases cited. But *cf.* Buckley v. Valeo, 424 U.S. 1, 113-18, 96 S.Ct. 612, 631 (1976). Not all legal scholars are opposed to having the Supreme Court render advisory opinions. See, *e.g.,* Note, *Case for an Advisory Function in the Federal Judiciary,* 50 Geo. L.J. 785 (1962); Note, *Advisory Opinions on the Constitutionality of Statutes,* 69 Harv. L. Rev. 1302 (1956); Aumann, *The Supreme Court and the Advisory Opinion,* 4 Ohio St. L.J. 21 (1937); but *cf.* Comment, *The State Advisory Opinion in Perspective,* 44 Ford L. Rev. 81 (1975); Frankfurter, *A Note on Advisory Opinions,* 37 Harv. L. Rev. 1002 (1924).

163. See H. Cummings and R. McFarland, Federal Justice 40, 81-92 (1937).

164. See, 1 K. Davis, Administrative Law Treatise § 4.09 (1958, Supp. 1970); 2 *id.* §§ 17.01-.09 (1958, Supp. 1970); Newman, *Should Official Advice be Reliable—Proposals as to Estoppel and Related Doctrines in Administrative Law,* 53 Colum. L. Rev. 374 (1953).

Notes

165. S. Res. 103, 75th Cong., 1st Sess., 81 Cong. Rec. 2804 (1937). See also, Davidson, *The Constitutionality and Utility of Advisory Opinions,* 2 U. of Toronto L.J. 254 (1938); Aumann, *The Supreme Court and the Advisory Opinion,* 4 Ohio St. L.J. 21 (1937); Comment, *The Advisory Opinion and the United States Supreme Court,* 5 Ford. L. Rev. 94 (1936); Arnold, *Trial by Combat and the New Deal,* 47 Harv. L. Rev. 913 (1934).

166. See letter of Chief Justice Hughes to Senator Wheeler, Chairman of the Senate Judiciary Committee, *reprinted in* H. Hart & H. Wechsler, The Federal Courts and the Federal System 43-44 n.58 (2d ed. P. Bator, P. Mishkin, D. Shapiro, & H. Wechsler 1973).

167. 392 U.S. 83, 97 (1968).

168. 365 U.S. 146, 157 (1961).

169. Compare De Funis v. Odegaard, 416 U.S. 312 (1974).

170. Flast v. Cohen, 392 U.S. 83, 97 (1968).

171. *Id.* at 97.

172. Barrows v. Jackson, 346 U.S. 249, 255 (1953). *Cf.* Ashwander v. Tennessee Valley Authority, 297 U.S. 288, 345-48 (1936) (Brandeis, J., concurring).

173. H. Hart and H. Wechsler, The Federal Courts and the Federal System 67 (2d ed. P. Bator, P. Mishkin, D. Shapiro, & H. Wechsler, 1973).

174. *Id.* at 66.

175. Clark, *Separation of Powers,* 11 Willamette L.J. 1 (1974). See also, Address by Attorney General Levi, Fourth Sulzbacher Memorial Lecture, Columbia Law School, Dec. 2, 1975 ("The branches of government were not designed to be at war with one another. The relationship was not to be an adversary one, though to think of it that way has become fashionable." *Id.* at 36.); Address by Judge Henry Friendly, Bicentennial Lecture Series, Dept. of Justice, Independence Hall, Philadelphia, Pa., Jan. 29, 1976, 20 (mimeograph); Levi, *Some Aspects of Separation of Powers,* 76 Colum. L. Rev. 371 (1976). See also Weinstein, *Rendering Advisory Opinions—Do We, Should We?* 54 Judicature 140 (1970); J.B. Weinstein, *The Role of the Chief Judge in A*

Modern System of Justice, in R.R. Wheeler and H.R. Whitcomb, Judicial Administration: Text and Readings 139, 145-46 (1977).

176. United States v. Nixon, 418 U.S. 683, 707, 94 S.Ct. 3090, 3107 (1974).

177. United States v. Cox, 342 F.2d 167, 190 (5th Cir.), *cert. denied,* 381 U.S. 935 (1965) (Wisdom, J., concurring).

178. U.S. News & World Report, March 31, 1975, at 28, col. 1. *Cf., e.g., Burger Accuses Congress of Lag on Court Reform, Hints Election-Year Politics Is Cause of Inaction on New Judgeships,* N.Y. Times, Feb. 16, 1976, at 1, col. 8. See also, *e.g.,* 1974 Cal. Judicial Council, Annual Rep. to Governor, ch. 1, pointing out the need to restructure the California Council on Criminal Justice to permit the judiciary to participate in planning criminal justice programs.

179. 424 U.S. 1, 96 S.Ct. 612, 683 (1976).

180. See Address by Attorney General Levi, Fourth Sulzbacher Memorial Lecture, Columbia Law School, December 2, 1975, in the Colum. L. Alumni Observer, Feb. 15, 1976, at 3 ("perhaps the ambiguities ought not be resolved.").

181. The historical materials are collected in H. Hart and H. Wechsler, The Federal Courts and the Federal System, 663, 682, 739, 749 (2d ed. P. Bator, P. Mishkin, D. Shapiro & H. Wechsler 1973). See also the discussion in Goldberg, *The Supreme Court, Congress and the Rules of Evidence,* 5 Seton Hall L. Rev. 667 (1974).

182. Act of Sept. 24, 1789, ch. 20, 1 Stat. 73.

183. See 1 J. Goebel, Jr., History of the Supreme Court of the United States 477-88 (1971).

184. *Id.* at 499.

185. *Id.* at 498.

186. *Id.* at 487 (emphasis added).

187. *Id.* at 505.

188. *Id.* at 502.

189. *Id.* at 508, citing letter of Madison to Pendleton of Sept. 14, 1789, Ms. Madison Papers XII, 30 (Library of Congress).

190. Letter of Caleb Strong to Robert Treat Paine of April 23, 1790. Ms. of the Robert Treat Paine Papers (Massachusetts Historical Society), *in* 1 J. Goebel, Jr., History of the Supreme Court of the United States 541 (1971).

191. *Id.* at 545.

192. Act of May 8, 1792, ch. 36 § 2, 1 Stat. 275.

193. Ms. Minutes of the U.S. Sup. Ct. of August 8, 1792 (National Archives), cited in 1 J. Goebel, Jr., History of the Supreme Court of the United States 547 (1971). See also G. Pellew, John Jay 239-40 (1899); 2 U.S. (2 Dall.) 359 (1792).

194. 1 J. Goebel, Jr., History of the Supreme Court of the United States 550-51 (1971).

195. Act of March 2, 1793, ch. 22 § 7, 1 Stat. 333.

196. Act of Aug. 23, 1842, ch. 188 § 6, 5 Stat. 516. See also, 13 Rev. Stat. § § 913, 917, 918 (1878).

197. 28 U.S.C. § 2075 (1970).

198. 28 U.S.C. § 2072 (1970).

199. 18 U.S.C. § § 3771, 3772 (1970).

200. 28 U.S.C.A. § 2076 (Supp. 1976).

201. Process Act of Sept. 29, 1789, ch. 21 § 2, 1 Stat. 93.

202. Act of May 8, 1792, ch. 36 § 2, 1 Stat. 275.

203. *Id.*

204. 20 U.S. (7 Wheat) xvii (1822).

205. 1. How. xli. It acted pursuant to the sweeping rule-making powers granted to it by the Act of August 23, 1842, ch. 188 § 6, 5 Stat. 516.

206. 226 U.S. 627 (1912).

207. See Lane, *Twenty Years Under the Federal Equity Rules,* 46 Harv. L. Rev. 638 (1933).

208. See generally Griswold & Mitchell, *The Narrative Record in Federal Equity Appeals,* 42 Harv. L. Rev. 483 (1929); Payne, *Counterclaims Under New Federal Equity Rule 30,* 10 Va. L. Rev. 598 (1924); Lane, *Federal Equity Rules,* 35 Harv. L. Rev. 276

(1922); Talley, *The New and the Old Federal Equity Rules Compared,* 18 Va. L. Rev. 663 (1913); H. Hart & H. Wechsler, Federal Courts and the Federal System 664-65 (2d ed. P. Bator, P. Mishkin, D. Shapiro & H. Wechsler 1973).

209. Act of Sept. 29, 1789, ch. 21 § 2, 1 Stat. 93.

210. Act of May 8, 1792, ch. 36 § 2, 1 Stat. 275.

211. Act of Aug. 23, 1842, ch. 188 § 6, 5 Stat. 516.

212. 44 U.S. (3 How.) ix (1844).

213. 254 U.S. 671 (1921).

214. 383 U.S. 1029 (1916).

215. The Federal Rules of Civil Procedure do contain a supplemental list of special admiralty rules. See Fed. R. Civ. Pro., Rules 9(h), 14(a), 14(c), 38(e), 82, Supp. Rules A-F. Prize proceedings are governed by 10 U.S.C. §§ 7651-81 (1970), pursuant to Rule 81(a). See generally H. Hart & H. Wechsler, Federal Courts and the Federal System 666-67 (2d ed. P. Bator, P. Mishkin, D. Shapiro & H. Wechsler 1973).

216. Act of July 1, 1898, ch. 541, 30 Stat. 544.

217. Chandler Act, June 22, 1938, ch. 575, 52 Stat. 840 (1938).

218. The bankruptcy laws are compiled in Title 11, U.S.C.

219. 172 U.S. 653 (1898).

220. 305 U.S. 677 (1939).

221. 411 U.S. 989, 93 S.Ct. 3095, effective Oct. 1, 1975.

222. Act of Sept. 24, 1789, ch. 20 § 34, 1 Stat. 73, 13 Rev. Stat. § 721 (1878), 28 U.S.C. § 725 (1940), amended 28 U.S.C. § 1652 (1970).

223. Act of Sept. 29, 1789, ch. 21 § 2, 1 Stat. 93.

224. See also Act of March 2, 1793, ch. 22 § 7, 1 Stat. 333.

225. See, *e.g.*, Process Act of May 19, 1828, ch. 68, 4 Stat. 278 (required federal courts to follow the procedure of the state courts in force on the effective date of the act when entering writs of execution and other orders of final judgment; state procedure in effect on the effective date made rule for proceeding before

judgment in courts sitting in states admitted after 1789); Act of August 1, 1842, ch. 109, 5 Stat. 499 (courts in states admitted after last Process Act required to follow state procedures in effect on effective date of act).

226. Act of Aug. 23, 1842, ch. 188 § 6, 5 Stat. 516.

227. Act of June 1, 1872, ch. 255, 17 Stat. 196.

228. *Id.* § 5.

229. See, *e.g.*, Clark & Moore, *A New Federal Civil Procedure*, 44 Yale L.J. 387, 401-11 (1935); Herron v. Southern Pacific, 283 U.S. 91 (1931); McDonald v. Pless, 238 U.S. 264 (1915); *Hearings on S. 2061 Before a Subcomm. of the Senate Comm. on the Judiciary*, 68th Cong., 1st Sess. 54 (1924) (remarks of Justice Sutherland).

230. See generally Sutherland, *The Grant of Rule-Making Power to the Supreme Court of the United States*, 32 Mich. L. Rev. 1116 (1934).

231. There is some indication that doubts about the courts' powers to enact simple rules of procedure led Chief Justice Hughes, aided by Attorney General Homer Cummings and others, to seek a formal delegation from Congress. P.G. Fish, The Politics of Federal Judicial Administration 62-65 (1973); see also, *Id.* at 20-21.

232. Clark & Moore, *A New Federal Civil Procedure*, 44 Yale L.J. 387, 388-89 (1935).

233. Act of June 19, 1934, ch. 651, 48 Stat. 1064. *Cf.* 28 U.S.C. § 2072 (1970). See also 78 Cong. Rec. 9362-63 (Senate Floor debate); 78 Cong. Rec. 10866 (House Floor debate); S. Rep. No. 1048, 73d Cong. 2d Sess. (1934); H.R. Rep. No. 1829, 73d Cong., 2d Sess. (1934).

234. Act of June 19, 1934, ch. 651, 48 Stat. 1064.

235. *Id.*

236. *Id.*

237. 13 Am. Law Inst. Proc. 61.

238. Order of June 3, 1935, 295 U.S. 774.

239. See 308 U.S. 645-766.

240. See 308 U.S. 642 (1939); 329 U.S. 839 (1947); 335 U.S. 919 (1948); 341 U.S. 959 (1951).

241. 28 U.S.C. § 331 (1970). See Clark, *The Role of the Supreme Court in Federal Rule-Making,* 46 J. Am. Jud. Soc'y 250, 253 (1963).

242. See, 28 U.S.C. § 2072 (Supp. V 1966), amending 28 U.S.C. § 2072 (1964), for origin of power to formulate appellate rules.

243. See, *e.g.,* concerning work of the Advisory Committee on Civil Rules, 368 U.S. 1009 (1961); 374 U.S. 861 (1963); 383 U.S. 1029 (1966); 389 U.S. 1121 (1968); 398 U.S. 977 (1970); *Advisory Committee's Explanatory Statement Concerning Amendments of the Discovery Rules,* 48 F.R.D. 487 (1970); Maris, *Federal Procedural Rule-Making: The Program of the Judicial Conference,* 47 A.B.A.J. 772 (1961); Kaplan, *Continuing Work of the Civil Committee: 1966 Amendments of the Federal Rules of Civil Procedure,* 81 Harv. L. Rev. 356, 591 (1967, 1968); Kaplan, *Amendments of the Federal Rules of Civil Procedure, 1961-1963,* 77 Harv. L. Rev. 601, 801 (1964).

244. 394 U.S. 286 (1969).

245. 28 U.S.C. § 1651 (1970).

246. H. Hart & H. Wechsler, The Federal Courts and the Federal System 1435 (2d ed. P. Bator, P. Mishkin, D. Shapiro, & H. Wechsler 1973).

247. Rules Governing Sections 2254 and 2255 Cases in the Federal Courts, eff. February 1, 1977, P.L. 94-426, 94-577 (1976); Letter of Judge Maris, January 31, 1973; 93 S.Ct. temp. ed. June 15, 1973, p. 1. See the fine critical article, Clinton, *Rule 9 of the Federal Habeas Corpus Rules: A Casestudy of the Need for Reform of the Rules Enabling Acts,* 63 Iowa L. Rev. (1977).

248. H. Hart & H. Wechsler, The Federal Courts and the Federal System 667 (2d ed. P. Bator, P. Mishkin, D. Shapiro, & H. Wechsler 1973).

249. See Act of February 24, 1933, ch. 119, 47 Stat. 904, as amended by Act of March 8, 1934, ch. 49, 48 Stat. 399. *Cf.* 18 U.S.C. § 3772 (1970).

250. 292 U.S. 661 (1934).

251. Act of June 29, 1940, ch. 445, 54 Stat. 688. See also, 18 U.S.C. § 3771 (1970).

252. 323 U.S. 821 (1944).

253. 327 U.S. 821 (1946).

254. See 335 U.S. 917, 949 (1948); 346 U.S. 941 (1954); 350 U.S. 1017 (1956); 383 U.S. 1087 (1966); 389 U.S. 1125 (1968); 401 U.S. 1025 (1971); 406 U.S. 983 (1972); 415 U.S. 1056 (1974).

255. 416 U.S. 1001 (1974).

256. 18 U.S.C. § 3771 (Supp. IV 1974) (enacted as Act of July 30, 1974, Pub. L. 93-361, 88 Stat. 397).

257. Act of July 31, 1975, Pub. L. 94-64, § 2, 89 Stat. 370.

258. Hungate, *Changes in the Rules of Criminal Procedure*, 61 A.B.A.J. 1203 (1975).

259. 389 U.S. 1063 (1968).

260. Committee on Rules of Practice and Procedure of the Judicial Conference of the United States, A Preliminary Report on the Advisability and Feasibility of Developing Uniform Rules of Evidence for the United States District Courts 3 (Feb. 1962) (footnotes omitted) (hereinafter cited as Preliminary Report on Evidence).

261. *Id.* at 12.

262. *Id.* at 1.

263. E. Morgan, J. Maguire & J. Weinstein, Cases and Materials on Evidence 258 (4th ed. 1957).

264. See, *e.g.*, Green, *The Admissibility of Evidence Under the Federal Rules*, 55 Harv. L. Rev. 197, 225 (1941); Estes, *The Need for Uniform Rules of Evidence in the Federal Courts*, 24 F.R.D. 331 (1960); *Report of the Special Cmt. on Uniform Evidence Rules for Fed. Cts. to the House of Delegates, American Bar Association*, 44 A.B.A.J. 1113 (1958).

265. Preliminary Report on Evidence at ix.

266. *Id.* at 29 (emphasis supplied). See *id.* at 32, n.125, *id.* at 35, n.138 for authority supporting this position.

267. *Id.* at 48-54.

268. (Mathew Bender ed. 1975) with cross references to Weinstein's Evidence.

269. *See* 1-5 J. Weinstein & M. Berger, Weinstein's Evidence (1975).

270. *See, e.g.,* the definition for this purpose in Weinstein, *Recognition in the United States of the Privilege of Another Jurisdiction,* 56 Colum. L. Rev. 535, 545 (1956); Weinstein, *The Uniformity-Conformity Dilemma Facing Draftsmen of Federal Rules of Evidence,* 69 Colum. L. Rev. 353 (1969); Goldberg (former Justice), *The Supreme Court, Congress and Rules of Evidence,* 5 Seton Hall L. Rev. 667, 684, n.89 (1974) ("Judge Weinstein categorizes evidentiary rules into three groups: Truth-determining rules, rules closely associated with particular substantive rights, and state evidence rules protecting extrinsic policy. Included in the third category are privileged communications."); Kaminsky, *States Evidentiary Privileges in Federal Civil Litigation,* 43 Fordham L. Rev. 923 (1975); Anderton, *The Constitutional and "Erie" Implications for Federal Diversity Cases of the Privilege Provisions of the Proposed Rules of Evidence,* 8 Lincoln L. Rev. 151 (1973); Krattenmaker, *Testimonial Privileges in Federal Courts: An Alternative to the Proposed Federal Rules of Evidence,* 62 Geo. L.J. 61 (1973) and other materials in 2 J. Weinstein & M. Berger, Weinstein's Evidence 501-11 (1975).
As indicated in the discussion of New Jersey's experience, III: A, *infra.,* the New Jersey courts' attempt to control rules of privilege independent of the legislature proved a failure. Yet the process seems to be repeating itself against what may be a more passive legislature in New Mexico. See New Mexico Rules of Evidence, Rule 501, discussed in III: A, *infra.*

271. *See, e.g.,* 2 J. Weinstein & M. Berger, Weinstein's Evidence ¶ 407[02] (1975) (remedial measures); *Id.* at ¶ 408[02] compromise); *Id.* at 3 ¶ 601[03], 601-20 to 601-21 (dead man statute); *Id.* at 1 ¶ 302[01] (presumptions); Blakey, *Substantive Use of Prior Inconsistent Statements Under the Federal Rules of Evidence,* 64 Ky. L.J. 3, 29 ff. (1975) (discussing effect of rule on forum shopping.).

272. 2 J. Weinstein & M. Berger, Weinstein's Evidence ¶ 501[01] (1975). See also Goldberg (former Justice), *The Supreme Court, Congress and Rules of Evidence,* 5 Seton Hall L. Rev. 667, 681-87 (1974).

273. Cong. Rec. 12254 (1974) (remarks of Rep. William L. Hungate).

274. See 2 J. Weinstein & M. Berger, Weinstein's Evidence ¶ 501[02] *et seq.* (1975); *Hearings on Amendments to Federal Rules of Criminal Procedure Before the Subcomm. on Criminal Justice of the House Comm. on the Judiciary,* 94th Cong., 1st Sess., ser. 6, at 129-30 (1975) ("a likely privilege [psychotherapist] to be recognized before the Supreme Court because the draft includes the privilege.").

275. 2 J. Weinstein & M. Berger, Weinstein's Evidence ¶ 501[02] *et seq.* (1975). See United States v. Mackey, 405 F. Supp. 854, 858 (E.D.N.Y. 1975); United States ex rel. Edney v. Smith, 425 F. Supp. 1038 (E.D.N.Y. 1976).

276. See, *e.g., Hearings on Proposed Rules of Evidence Before the Special Comm. on Reform of Federal Criminal Laws of the House Comm. on the Judiciary,*93d Cong., 1st Sess., ser. 2, at 142 ff. (testimony of Justice Arthur J. Goldberg), at 158 ff. (testimony on behalf of The Washington Council of Lawyers, see esp. pp. 159 ff. noting that not all material available to advisory committee was available to public, and special permission to review comments to the advisory committee from the public was needed; pp. 160-61, lack of "input" by civil liberty, dissident, poverty and minority groups and public defenders; pp. 161 ff. objection to unexplained changes between last published draft and rules promulgated by Supreme Court); pp. 246 ff. (testimony of Chief Judge Henry J. Friendly); pp. 392 ff. (testimony on behalf of Project on Corporate Responsibility); pp. 420 ff. (testimony on behalf of Public Citizen, Inc.); pp. 514-15 (communication from NAACP) (1973); *Hearings on Proposed Amendments to Federal Rules of Criminal Procedure Before the Subcomm. on Criminal Justice of the House Comm. on the Judiciary,* 93d Cong., 2d Sess., ser. 61, at 203 ff. (statement of Prof. Howard Lesnick) (1974).

277. The influence, for example, of Senator McClellan was obvious and is referred to repeatedly in 2 J. Weinstein & M. Berger, Weinstein's Evidence (1975). See his communications at *Hearings on Proposed Rules of Evidence Before the Special Subcomm. on Reform of Federal Criminal Laws of the House Comm. on the Judiciary,* 93d Cong., 1st Sess., ser. 2, at 312 ff. (1973).

278. Lesnick, *The Federal Rule-Making Process: A Time for Reexamination,* 61 A.B.A.J. 579, 581 (1975). *Cf.* P. Fish, The Politics of Federal Judicial Administration 71-72, 291-94 (1973).

279. See Hungate, *An Introduction to the Proposed Rules of Evidence,* 32 Fed. B.J. 225, 228-29 (1973).

280. See Rule 801(d)(1)(C) Pub. L. No. 94-113 (Oct. 16, 1975). Subsequent amendments were required to correct minor problems in the prior enactment. 89 Stat. 805, Pub. L. No. 94-149.

281. N.J. Const. art. VI, § 2, ¶ 3, "The Supreme Court shall make rules governing the administration of all courts in the State and, subject to law, the practice and procedure in all such courts."

282. 5 N.J. 240, 74 A.2d 406, *cert. denied,* 340 U.S. 877, 71 S.Ct. 123 (1950). See Kaplan & Greene, *The Legislature's Relation to Judicial Rule-Making: An Appraisal of Winberry v. Salisbury,* 65 Harv. L. Rev. 234 (1951). The New Jersey court continues to cite *Winberry* with approval. See American Trials Lawyers v. New Jersey Supreme Court, 66 N.J. 258, 330 A.2d 350, 352 (1974) (contingent fees). See also Note, *Prejudgment Interest Rule Upheld,* 27 Rutgers L. Rev. 345 (1974); Pound, *Procedure Under Rules of Court in New Jersey,* 66 Harv. L. Rev. 28 (1952); Levin & Amsterdam, *Legislative Control Over Judicial Rulemaking: A Problem in Constitutional Revision,* 107 U. Pa. L. Rev. 1 (1958). *Cf.* Columbia Lumber & Millwork Co. v. De Stefano, 12 N.J. 117, 95 A.2d 914 (1953) (*Winberry* applied to hold a statute in conflict with a court rule invalid).

283. 5 N.J. at 244, 74 A.2d at 408.

284. Kaplan & Greene, *The Legislature's Relation to Judicial Rule-Making: An Appraisal of Winberry v. Salisbury,* 65 Harv. L. Rev. 234, 247 (1951).

285. See, *e.g.,* Sofaer, *Executive Privilege: An Historical Note,* 75 Colum. L. Rev. 1318 (1975).

286. Ashman, *Measuring the Judicial Rule-Making Power,* 59 J. Am. Jud. Soc'y. 215, 219 (1975). The comment is based upon a comprehensive nationwide survey, American Judicature Society, Uses of Judicial Rule-Making Power (mimeograph 1974).

287. Kaplan & Greene, *The Legislature's Relation to Judicial Rule-Making: An Appraisal of Winberry v. Salisbury,* 65 Harv. L. Rev. 234, 247 (1951).

288. See, *e.g.*, Grant v. Curtin, 71 A.2d 304 (Md. 1950).

289. See, *e.g.*, Sniadach v. Family Finance Corporation, 395 U.S. 337, 89 S.Ct. 1820, 23 L.Ed.2d 349 (1969) (statutory garnishment proceedings invalid).

290. Kaplan & Greene, *The Legislature's Relation to Judicial Rule-Making: An Appraisal of Winberry v. Salisbury*, 65 Harv. L. Rev. 234, 251 (1951).

291. Wigmore, *All Legislative Rules for Judiciary Procedure are Void Constitutionally*, 23 Ill. L. Rev. 276 (1928) reprinted 20 J. Am. Jud. Soc'y 159 (1936); *cf.* Pound, *The Rule Making Power of the Courts*, 12 A.B.A.J. 599, 600 (1926).

292. Kaplan & Greene, *The Legislature's Relation to Judicial Rule-Making: An Appraisal of Winberry v. Salisbury*, 65 Harv. L. Rev. 234, 254 (1951).

293. *See, e.g.*, Cohn v. Borchard Affiliations, 30 App. Div.2d 74, 289 N.Y.S.2d 771 (1st Dept. 1968), *rev'd*, 25 N.Y.2d 237, 303 N.Y.S.2d 633 (1969) (provision governing dismissal for failure to prosecute invalid), noted 43 N.Y.U.L. Rev. 776 (1968) (the note is critical of the lower court decision); State v. Clemente, 36 Conn. L.J. No. 1, at 1 (July 2, 1974), strongly criticized in Kay, *The Rule-Making Authority and Separation of Powers in Connecticut*, 8 Conn. L. Rev. 1 (1975); R.E.W. Const. Co., v. District Court, 88 Idaho 426, 400 P.2d 390 (1965), criticized in 8 Idaho L. Rev. 379 (1972) and 29 Wash & Lee L. Rev. 164 (1972); Agran v. Checker Taxi Co., 412 Ill. 145, 105 N.E.2d 713 (1952); State v. Smith, 8 Wash.2d 498, 527 P.2d 674 (1974); Slate v. Bridenhager, 257 Ind. 699, 279 N.E.2d 794 (1972); Newell v. State, 308 So.2d 71 (Miss. 1975).

294. 36 Conn L.J. No. 1 at 1 (July 2, 1974).

295. Jencks v. United States, 353 U.S. 657, 77 S.Ct. 1007, 1 L.Ed.2d 1103 (1957) (decided under power of court to control federal procedure). The act was approved as a lawful exercise of congressional power to control the subject. Palermo v. United States, 360 U.S. 343, 80 S.Ct. 41 (1959).

296. Kay, *The Rule-Making Authority and Separation of Powers in Connecticut*, 8 Conn. L. Rev. 1, 22 (1974).

297. *Id.* at 43.

298. Effective July 1, 1973 (emphasis supplied). By contrast, Rule 501 of the Federal Rules acknowledges the legislature's power. So do the rules of most states that use the Federal Rules of Evidence as a model: Florida, Rule 50.501; Maine Rule 501; Nebraska Section 22 Evidence Act; Nevada Section 49.015 of NRS; Wisconsin Rule 905.01.

299. See N.M. Stat. Ann. § 20-1-12(c)(1953) (accountant); N.M. Stat Ann. § 20-1-12.1 (1953) (news sources); N.M. Stat. Ann. § 54-11-39 (1953) (medical research); N.M. Stat. Ann § 67-30-17 (1953) (certified psychologist).

300. This assumption is based upon conversations by the author with members of the bench, bar, and legislature of New Mexico. See Ammerman v. Hubbard Broadcasting, Inc., 551 P. 2d 1354 (N.M. 1976) (striking down newsperson's privilege); 2 J.B. Weinstein & M.A. Berger, Weinstein's Evidence, 49-50 (1976 Supp.). It is suggested that, were the New Mexico legislature intent on making an issue of the matter, as by adoption of a new reporter's privilege statute, the court could easily find a way of escaping from the apparent position it has placed itself in, which is contrary to that in this country and England.

301. *See, e.g.*, Board of Com'rs of the Alabama State Bar v. State ex rel. Baxley, 324 So.2d 256 (Ala. 1976).

302. *See, e.g.*, Mildner v. Gulotta, et al., 405 F.Supp. 182, 201 (E.D.N.Y. 1975) (dissent), *aff'd*, 425 U.S. 901, 96 Sup.Ct. 1489 (1976).

303. N.J. Const., art VI, Sec. 2, ¶ 3.

304. See, *e.g.*, *How Shall the Proposed Code of Evidence be Adopted*, 78 N.J.L.J. 316 (1955); *Report on Manner of Adopting Proposed Evidence Code*, 78 *Id.* (1955) (reporting suggestion of Essex County Bar Association that the legislature and then the Court adopt the same provisions as a way out of the impasse); *Interim Announcement of the Legislative Commission to Study Improvement of the Law of Evidence*, 79 *Id.* 97 (1956) (reporting appointment of Legislative Commission to study subject); Kean, *An Analysis of the Report of the Legislative Commission to Study the Improvement of the Law of Evidence*, 79 *Id.* 469, (1956); *Evidence Revision by Cooperation*, 79 *Id.* 496, (1956) (editorial calling for cooperation); *Vanderbilt Critical of Evidence Bill*, 80 *Id.* 205 (1957); *Bigelow Urges Codification of Evidence Rule*, 80

Id. 205 (1957); *Statement by Josiah Stryker at Legislative Hearing on Evidence Revision,* 80 *Id.* 211 (1957); *Milton Submits Comments on Evidence Revision,* 80 *Id.* 241 (1957); *Codification of Evidence Law Favored by Unanimous Vote of State Bar Association,* 80 *Id.* 253 (1957); *Statement of Milton T. Lasher, President of New Jersey State Bar Association, Concerning the Proposed Evidence Code,* 80 *Id.* 269 (1957); *Evidence Reform and Timing,* 80 *Id.* 269 (1957); 84 *Id.* 86, February 16, 1961 (Governor suggests constitutional revision). See also Morgan, *Practical Difficulties Impeding Reform in the Law of Evidence,* 14 Vand. L. Rev. 725, 736 (1961); Brooks, *Evidence,* 14 Rutgers L. Rev. 390 (1960); Tyree, *Evidence,* 10 Rutgers L. Rev. 324 (1956).

305. 5 N.J. 240, 74 A.2d 406, *cert. denied,* 340 U.S. 877 (1950).

306. L. 1960, c. 52, p. 461, § 33; (codified at N.J.S.A. 2A:84A-33 (Supp. 1975)).

307. N.J.S.A. 2A:84A-34 (Supp. 1974).

308. N.J.S.A. 2A:84A-35 (Supp. 1974).

309. L. 1965, c. 56 § 2, as amended by L. 1966, c. 184, § 2; L. 1967, c. 3 § 1. (codified at N.J.S.A. 2A:84A-36 (Supp. 1975)).

310. L. 1968, c. 183, § 1, eff. July 19, 1968. (codified at N.J.S.A. 2A:84A-39.1 (Supp. 1975)).

311. L. 1970, c. 258, § 2, eff. Nov. 2, 1970 (codified at N.J.S.A. 2A:84A-39.1 (Supp. 1975)).

312. See, *e.g.,* Note, *The Rule-Making Powers of the Illinois Supreme Court,* 1965 U. of Ill. L.F. 903, 906.

313. See Busik v. Levine, 63 N.J. 351, 307 A.2d 571 (1973), noted Rutgers L. Rev. 345 (1974).

314. Lynch, *The New Jersey Supreme Court and the Counsel Fees Rule: Procedure or Substance and Remedy,* 4 Seton Hall L. Rev. 19, 421, 496 (1973).

315. Note, *The Rulemaking Power of the Florida Supreme Court: The Twilight Zone Between Substance and Procedure,* 24 U. Fla. L. Rev. 87, 91 (1971).

316. *Id.* at 105. See also Jacob memorandum at ¶ 8: "the policy which is followed [by the English Supreme Court Rule

Committee] is to avoid making a rule the validity of which *may* be in doubt." (Emphasis in original.)

317. *See, e.g.,* Ashman, *Measuring the Judicial Rule-Making Power,* 59 J. Am. Jud. Soc'y 215 (1975).

318. Tate, *The Rule-Making Power of the Courts in Louisiana,* 24, La. L. Rev. 555, 568 (1964).

319. If rule-making power were granted the courts, Judge Tate suggested that the legislature retain general supervisory power. "In the future, a less progressive court system might take too parochial a view of the regulation of judicial procedure, a matter which is after all the concern of our entire people, not just of the bench and bar." *Id.*

320. See Ashman, *Measuring the Judicial Rule-Making Power,* 59 J. Am. Jud. Soc'y 215, 219 (1975). See the full and excellent survey in American Judicature Society, Uses of the Judicial Rule-Making Power (mimeograph 1974).

321. See Nelson, *The Reform of Common Law Pleading in Massachusetts 1760-1830: Adjudication as a Prelude to Legislation,* 122 U. Pa. L. Rev. 97, 98 (1973).

322. See, *e.g.,* C. Clark, Handbook of the Law of Code Pleading 17-19 (1928); Pound, David Dudley Field: An Appraisal in David Dudley Field: Centenary Essays 1 (1949); Kaplan & Greene, *The Legislature's Relation to Judicial Rule-Making: An Appraisal of Winberry v. Salisbury,* 65 Harv. L. Rev. 234, 252 (1951).

323. N.Y.C.P.A. § 374a, superseded by N.Y.C.P.L.R. 4518 (McKinney 1963); 28 U.S.C. § 1732 (1971).

324. Lasky v. State Farm Ins. Co., 296 So.2d 9 (Fla. 1974) (unconstitutional in part); Manzanares v. Bell, 522 P.2d 1291 (Kan. 1974); Opinion of the Justices, 304 A.2d 881 (N.H. 1973) (unconstitutional in part); Grace v. Howlett, 283 N.E.2d 474 (Ill. 1972) (unconstitutional); Pinnick v. Cleary, 271 N.E.2d 592 (Mass. 1971); N.Y. Ins. Law §§ 670-77 (McKinney Supp. 1975); Pa. Stat. Ann. tit. 40 §§ 1009.101-.701 (Supp. 1976).

325. A. Vanderbilt, Minimum Standards of Judicial Administration 514 (1949).

326. *Id.* at 92. Emphasis in original. See also *id.* at 137.

327. 5 N.J. 240, 74 A.2d 406, *cert. denied,* 340 U.S. 877 (1950).

328. Vanderbilt admitted that "local rules" may be superseded by statute. A. Vanderbilt, Minimum Standards of Judicial Administration 93-94 (1949). He also agreed that, "In no state is rule-making power exercised over other courts without some specific authorization, either constitutional or statutory." *Id.* at 94.

329. ABA Comm. on Standards of Judicial Administration, Standards Relating to Court Organization 64 (Tent. Draft 1973); see also, *e.g.,* Sunderland, *Implementing the Rule-making Power,* 25 N.Y.U.L. Rev. 27 (1950).

330. A. Vanderbilt, Minimum Standards of Judicial Administration 128 (1949).

331. Advisory Committee on Practice & Procedure, Third Preliminary Report 883 n.41 (N.Y. Leg. Doc. No. 17, 1959) (Weinstein, Reporter).
This is the practice, for example, in Pennsylvania. Philip W. Amram, Chairman of the Supreme Court of Pennsylvania Civil Procedural Rules Committee for many years in a letter to the author dated February 14, 1977, summarizes the Pennsylvania practice as follows:

[W]e have, for years, adopted the policy that all proposed new rules or amendments (other than trifling technical amendments) are proposed as Recommendations which are published in the Pennsylvania Bulletin and also distributed through the Pennsylvania Bar Association and all local bar associations for comment and criticism before we submit anything to the Supreme Court for promulgation.

In Pennsylvania we have no legislative veto and the rule-making power of the Supreme Court is constitutional. We recognize a certain amount of county autonomy in minor areas, particularly because of the difference between big city practice in Philadelphia and Pittsburgh and small town and rural practice in other counties of the state. Nevertheless, we keep these local variations to an absolute minimum since we have statewide practice and lawyers practising in other counties should not be tripped up by local variances in significant matters.

Used by permission of the author.

332. Some statutes do provide for periodic hearings at which objections may be voiced and specific suggestions made. *Id.* at 833, n.43.

333. See, J. Parness & C. Korbakes, A Study of the Procedural Rule-Making Power in the United States, App. III (Am. Judicature Soc'y mimeo. 1973).

334. ABA Comm. on Standards of Judicial Administration, Standards Relating to Court Organization 63 (Tent. Draft 1973).

335. California Law Revision Commission, Recommendation Proposing an Evidence Code 3-4 (1965). See, *e.g.,* the extensive and excellent studies on evidence by Professor Chadbourn and others in 6 California Law Revision Commission, Reports, Recommendations and Studies 1962-1964; California Law Revision Commission, Recommendation Proposing an Evidence Code (1965). See also B. Witkin, California Evidence § § 5-6 (2d ed. 1966). The California Law Revision Commission consists of one member of the Senate, one of the Assembly and seven appointed by the Governor with the advice and consent of the Senate. Cal. Gov't Code § 10301 (West 1966).

336. California Law Revision Commission, Recommendation Proposing an Evidence Code 3, 5 (1965).

337. *Id.* at 5-8.

338. *Id.* at 5.

339. See 1 B. Witkin, California Procedure § 119-20, 52-53, 126-33 (2d ed. 1970).

340. Cal. Gov't Code § 68070 (West 1964).

341. The New York Judicial Conference consists of the Chief Judge of the State of New York, the four presiding justices, one from each of the departments of the appellate division, a justice of the Supreme Court from each of the four departments, and judges representing the surrogates courts, county courts, court of claims, family court, Criminal Court of the City of New York and Civil Court of the City of New York. The following ex officio members by statute attend meetings of the Conference and make recommendations: the chairman and ranking minority member of the Judiciary Committee of the Senate and of the Assembly and the chairman and ranking minority member of the Codes Committee

of the Senate and Assembly. The state administrator acts as secretary assisted by the counsel, administration officer, and extensive staff. Judicial Conference of the State of New York, Report to the Administrative Board, 16 Ann. Rep. 9-10, A-2 ff. (Leg. Doc. No. 90, 1971).

342. *See, e.g.,* Judicial Conference of the State of New York, Report to the 1976 Legislature in relation to the Civil Practice Law and Rules and Proposed Amendments Adopted Pursuant to Section 229 of the Judiciary Law (mimeograph Feb. 1, 1976) (studies and recommendations on notice of claim, attachment, replevin, arrest, and receivership; videotaping depositions; direct actions against liability insurance carriers, etc.).

343. Advice to the Judicial Conference is by the Committee to Advise and Consult with the Judicial Conference on the C.P.L.R., consisting of leading members of the bar and law teaching profession. The recommendations of this group are based upon extensive studies, usually prepared by law professors. Its recommendations are generally followed in amendments to the rules of the C.P.L.R. and, often, by the legislature in proposals to amend sections of the C.P.L.R. and related statutes. See, *e.g.,* Judicial Conference of the State of New York, Report of the Administrative Board, 16 Ann. Rep. A-28 ff. (Leg. Doc. No. 90, 1971).

Revision of the New York law of evidence is being undertaken by the New York Law Revision Commission rather than by the Judicial Conference. Recommendations of the commission are normally embodied in statutes, not in rules.

344. Comm'n on Revision of the Fed. Ct. App. System, Structure and Internal Procedures: Recommendations for Change, A Preliminary Report 61 (1975).

345. *Id.*

346. Levin & Amsterdam, *Legislative Control Over Judicial Rule-Making: A Problem in Constitutional Revision,* 107 U. Pa. L. Rev. 1, 42 (1958).

347. 10 Wheat.1 (1825).

348. *Id.* at 21-22.

349. See also Bank of the United States v. Halstead, 23 U.S. (10 Wheat.) 51, 53 (1825); Beers v. Haughton, 34 U.S. (9 Pet.) 215, 235, 236 (1835).

350. 312 U.S. 1, 9-10, 61 S.Ct. 422, 424, 85 L.Ed. 479 (1941).

351. *Id.* at 14-15, 61 S.Ct. at 424, 85 L.Ed. 479.

352. *Id.* at 18, 61 S.Ct. at 428, 85 L.Ed. 479 (Frankfurter, J., dissenting).

353. *See, e.g.,* Panama Refining Co. v. Ryan, 293 U.S. 388, 415, 421, 430, 55 S.Ct. 241, 246, 248-49, 252-53, 79 L.Ed. 446 (1935) ("We look to the statute to see whether the Congress has declared a policy with respect to that subject"); United States v. Chicago, Milwaukee, St. Paul & Pacific R. Co., 282 U.S. 311, 324, 51 S.Ct. 159, 162, 75 L.Ed. 350 (1931) ("Congress cannot delegate any part of its legislative power except under the limitation of a prescribed standard. . . ."); Yakus v. United States, 321 U.S. 414, 426, 64 S.Ct. 660, 668, 88 L.Ed. 884 (1944) (there is an unlawful delegation only where "there is an absence of standards for the guidance of the Administration's action, so that it would be impossible in a proper proceeding to ascertain whether the will of Congress has been obeyed"); Wayman v. Southard, 23 U.S. (10 Wheat.) 1, 41-42, 6 L.Ed. 253 (1825) (Congress must decide the important policy questions; the delegate could fill in the details).

354. See Schechter Poultry Corp. v. United States, 295 U.S. 495, 55 S.Ct. 837, 79 L.Ed. 1570 (1935); Panama Refining Co. v. Ryan, 293 U.S. 388, 55 S.Ct. 241, 79 L.Ed. 446 (1935). *Cf.* B. Bellush, The Failure of the NRA 168 (1975).

355. *See* Jaffe, An Essay on Delegation of Legislative Power, I and II, 47 Colum. L. Rev. 359, 561 (1947); K. Davis, Administrative Law Treatise § 2.01-.06 (1958).

356. See Gewirtz, *The Courts, Congress and Executive Policy-Making,* 39 L. & Contemp. Problems (1976) (in publication). *See also* A. Schlesinger, Jr., The Imperial Presidency (1973); Freedman, *Crisis and Legitimacy in the Administrative Process,* 27 Stan. L. Rev. 1041 (1975).

357. 23 U.S. (10 Wheat.), 6 L.Ed. 253 (1825).

358. 18 U.S.C. § 3006A (g); 28 U.S.C. §§ 753, 1825, 2249, 2250. See note 247, *supra.*

359. 424 U.S. 1, 96 S.Ct. 612 (1976).

360. 323 U.S. 821, 822 (1944). Much the same objection was made of the English Rules Committee. See Evershed Committee, Second Interim Report (Cmnd. 8176, 1915), ¶¶ 132-39: "the existing Committee although impressive in point of distinction is somewhat far removed from the workaday affairs of administration of the Rules." Quoted in Jacob Memorandum, ¶ 4.

361. *See, e.g.,* 368 U.S. 1012 (1961); 374 U.S. 865 (1963); 383 U.S. 1032 (1966); 383 U.S. 1089 (1966); 398 U.S. 979 (1970); 401 U.S. 1019 (1971).

362. 374 U.S. at 865-66, 869-70 (1963).

363. Mississippi Publishing Corp. v. Murphree, 326 U.S. 438, 444, 66 S.Ct. 242, 246, 90 L.Ed. 185 (1946). *Cf.,* Ragan v. Merchants Transfer & Warehouse Co., 337 U.S. 530, 69 S.Ct. 1233, 93 L.Ed. 520 (1949) (Fed. R. Civ. P. 3 held invalid).

364. 380 U.S. 460, 85 S.Ct. 1136, 14 L.Ed.2d 8 (1965).

365. *Id.* at 470, 85 S.Ct. at 1143, 14 L.Ed.2d 8.

366. *Id.* at 471, 85 S.Ct. at 1144, 14 L.Ed.2d 8.

367. H. Hart & H. Wechsler, The Federal Courts and The Federal System 748 (2d ed. P. Bator, P. Mishkin, D. Shapiro, & H. Wechsler 1973).

368. 380 U.S. at 474, 85 S.Ct. at 1145, 14 L.Ed.2d 8 (1965).

369. *Advisory Committee Note to Rule 501* in 2 J. Weinstein & M. Berger, Weinstein's Evidence 501-8 (1975).

370. See generally the discussion in *id.* at ¶ 501[01].

371. 4 Moore's Federal Practice ¶ 26.63[6] (1975).

372. *Id.* at 26-386.

373. 329 U.S. 495, 67 S.Ct. 385, 91 L.Ed. 451 (1947).

374. See 8 Wright & Miller, Federal Practice and Procedure: Civil §§ 2022, 2023 (1970).

375. 423 F.2d 487 (7th Cir. 1970) (per curiam), *aff'd by equally divided court,* 400 U.S. 955, 91 S.Ct. 479, 27 L.Ed.2d 433, *reh. denied,* 401 U.S. 950, 91 S.Ct. 917, 28 L.Ed.2d 234 (1971). See the history of the provision in 2 J. Weinstein & M. Berger, Weinstein's Evidence, ¶ 503[01], p. 503-14; ¶ 503(b)[04], p. 503-44 (1975).

Notes

376. 2 J. Weinstein & M. Berger, Weinstein's Evidence, ¶ 503[01], ¶ 503(b)[04] (1975). There were, of course, many other changes in the new draft.

377. *See, e.g.*, Myers, *The Attorney Client Relationship and the Code of Professional Responsibility: Suggested Attorney Liability for Breach of Duty to Disclose Fraud to the Securities and Exchange Commission*, 44 Ford. L. Rev. 1113 (1976); Policy of ABA on lawyers' responses to auditors; Glasser, *Bar's Responses to Auditors: New Policies, Few Concessions*, N.Y.L.J., Jan. 19, 1976, at 1, col. 3; see also, as to some of the complexities and the relationship to problems of ethics, Rotunda, *Book Review*, 89 Harv. L. Rev. 662 (1976).

378. See 2 J. Weinstein & M. Berger, Weinstein's Evidence, ¶ 510[01], pp. 510-17 to -18, ¶ 510[06], ¶ 510[07] (1975).

379. Lumbard, Criminal Justice and the Rule-Making Power, Address to Conference of Chief Justices, Honolulu, Aug. 3, 1967, at 9 (mimeograph).

380. *Id.*

381. P. Fish, The Politics of Federal Judicial Administration 241 (1973). See also the criticism of former Justice Goldberg in *The Supreme Court, Congress, and Rules of Evidence*, 5 Seton Hall L. Rev. 667 (1974).

382. Lesnick, *The Federal Rule-Making Process: A Time for Re-examination*, 61 A.B.A.J. 579-80 (1975). Reprinted by permission. See also statement by H. Lesnick on behalf of Washington Council of Lawyers, *Hearings on Proposed Amendments to Federal Rules of Criminal Procedure Before the Subcomm. on Criminal Justice of the House Comm. on the Judiciary*, 93d Cong., 2d Sess. ser. 61, at 197-209 (1974).

The suggestion of Friedenthal that the Supreme Court exercise "more diligence" in reviewing the rules is unrealistic in view of the Court's heavy workload. See Friedenthal, *The Rulemaking Power of the Supreme Court: A Contemporary Crisis*, 27 Stan. L. Rev. 673, 685 (1975).

On constitutional grounds a student note suggests leaving general rule-making with the Supreme Court, but encouraging the Judicial Conference to recommend "substantive" changes, such as those dealing with privileges, to Congress. Note, *Separation of Powers and the Federal Rules of Evidence*, 26 Hastings L. J. 1059

(1975). This is a useful suggestion in other areas, as, for example, proposals to provide for review of sentences. See addendum to Preface, *supra*. Cf. Note, *Federal Rules of Evidence*, 49 Wash. L. Rev. 1184 (1974) (presumptions and privileges beyond power of courts to affect by rules). See also the thoughtful critical analysis in Clinton, note 247, *supra*.

383. *Id.* at 580-83.

384. The further point that Professor Lesnick makes that "the appropriateness of the extreme centralization of authority in the chief justice should be examined," seems more doubtful. See Weinstein, *The Role of the Chief Judge in a Modern System of Justice*, Record of N.Y.C.B.A. 291 (1973). The present Chief Justice, Warren Burger, has devoted an enormous amount of energy to improving judicial administration. The author's observations of his work in a number of committees and at various official meetings, suggests that the Chief Justice's leadership role has been useful and that this aspect of his work should not be limited.

385. *Id.* at 583.

386. *Id.* at 584.

387. 28 U.S.C.A. § 2076 (Supp. 1976).

388. *Id.*

389. *Id.* See 5 J. Weinstein & M. Berger, Weinstein's Evidence, pp. 1102-4 to 1102-13 (1975) for the history of this provision.

390. 28 U.S.C. §§ 2072, 2075 (1970); 18 U.S.C. § 3771 (1970).

391. 18 U.S.C. § 3772 (1970).

392. Lesnick, *The Federal Rule-Making Process: A Time for Re-examination*, 61 A.B.A.J. 579, 583 (1975).

393. Hungate, *Changes in the Federal Rules of Criminal Procedure*, 61 A.B.A.J. 1203, 1207 (1975) ("we should accord a healthy respect to any amendment proposed by the Supreme Court."). H.R. 3413, 95th Cong., 1st Sess., has many admirable features, but the requirement that rules not take effect until "approved by Act of Congress" constitutes an unfortunate step in the wrong direction.

394. Hungate, *The Federal Rules of Criminal Procedure,* 1975 Case and Comment 17, 22 (Nov.-Dec.).

395. See statements of C. R. Halpern and G. T. Frampton, Jr., in *Hearings on Proposed Rules of Evidence Before the Special Subcomm. on Reform of Federal Criminal Laws of the House Comm. on the Judiciary,* 93d Cong. 1st Sess., at 168 (1973); statement by H. Lesnick on behalf of Washington Council of Lawyers, *Hearings on Proposed Amendments to Federal Rules of Criminal Procedure Before Subcomm. on Criminal Justice of the House Comm. on the Judiciary,* 93d Cong., 2d Sess., at 203 (1974).

396. 18 U.S.C.A. § § 3161-74 (1975) Pub. L. No. 93-619. The act is discussed in connection with local rules, *infra.*

397. *Hearings on Proposed Amendments to Federal Rules of Criminal Procedure Before the Subcomm. on Criminal Justice of the House Comm. on the Judiciary,* 93 Cong., 2d Sess., ser. 61, at 5-6 (1974).

398. See *Hearings on Proposed Amendments to Federal Rules of Criminal Procedure Before the Subcomm. on Criminal Justice of the House Comm. on the Judiciary,* 93d Cong., 2d Sess., ser. 61, at 207 (1974). *Cf.* suggestion of an independent commission in Lesnick, *The Federal Rule-Making Process: A Time for Re-examination,* 61 A.B.A.J. 579, 583 (1975).

399. See Clark, *The Role of the Supreme Court in Federal Rule-Making,* 46 J. Am. Jud. Soc'y 250, 256-57 (1963).

400. *Cf.* Oliver, *Reflections on the History of Circuit Judicial Councils and Circuit Judicial Conferences,* 64 F.R.D. 201, 212 (1975) ("[I]f effective and innovative procedures are ever to be designed for the improvement of the administration of justice on the trial court level, the suggestions for improvement will more likely come from trial judges and the trial Bar than from any other source.").

401. See Buckley v. Valeo, 424 U.S. 1, 124-27, 96 Sup. Ct. 612 (1976).

402. Emphasis supplied.

403. Buckley v. Valeo, 424 U.S. 1, 123 96 Sup. Ct. 612 (1976).

404. See, *e.g.,* Friendly, *Some Kind of Hearing,* 123 U. Pa. L. Rev. 1267, 1272-73, 1305 ff. (1975).

405. *Cf.* United States v. Florida E. Coast Ry., 410 U.S. 224, 93 S.Ct. 810, 35 L.Ed.2d 223 (1973).

406. Friendly, *Some Kind of Hearing,* 123 U. Pa. L. Rev. 1267, 1315 (1975).

407. Hungate, *Changes in the Federal Rules of Criminal Procedure,* 61 A.B.A.J. 1203, 1207 (1975).

408. Ch. 22, § 7, 1 Stat. 335.

409. See also Act of May 8, 1792, ch. 36, § 2, 1 Stat. 276; Judiciary Act of 1789, ch. 20, § 17, 1 Stat. 83. See Wayman v. Southard, 23 U.S. (10 Wheat.) 1, 6 L.Ed. 253 (1825) (Marshall, Ch. J., constitutional); Cooke v. Avery, 147 U.S. 375, 13 S. Ct. 340, 37 L.Ed. 209 (1893) (same); Shepard v. Adams, 168 U.S. 618, 625, 18 S.Ct. 214, 216, 42 L.Ed. 602 (1898) (wide discretion); The Columbia, 100 F. 890 (E.D.N.Y. 1900) (admiralty); Note, *Rule 83 and the Local Federal Rules,* 67 Colum. L. Rev. 1251, 1253-54 (1967).

410. See, *e.g.,* Act of June 1, 1872, ch. 255, § 5, 17 Stat. 197; Chisholm v. Gilmer, 299 U.S. 99, 57 S.Ct. 65, 81 L.Ed. 63 (1936).

411. See also such specific grants as 28 U.S.C. §§ 137, 139-41, 751-54, 1654, 1863(b), 1914(c) (1970), and the Speedy Trial Act, 18 U.S.C.A. § 3165 (1975).

412. See also the specific grants in Fed. R. Civ. P. 16, 40, 66, and 78; Fed. R. App. P. 47; and Fed. R. Crim. P. 57(a) and 50(b), which requires adoption of local speedy trial rules.

413. *See, e.g.,* Shotkin v. Westinghouse Elec. & Mfg. Co., 169 F.2d 825, 826 (10th Cir. 1948) (power to dismiss for want of prosecution); United States v. Furey, 514 F.2d 1098, 1103 (2d Cir. 1975) (speedy trial rule in criminal cases).

414. Advisory Committee on Practice & Procedure, Third Preliminary Report 832 n.33 (N.Y. Leg. Doc. No. 17, 1959) (Weinstein, Reporter).

415. For example, in Doran v. United States, 475 F.2d 742, 743 (1st Cir. 1973) (per curiam) there is a discussion of the need

for keeping the local rules up-to-date and for arranging for their distribution.

416. Comment, *The Local Rules of Civil Procedure in the Federal District Courts—A Survey,* 1966 Duke L.J. 1011, 1012, See also Note, *Rule 83 and the Local Federal Rules,* 67 Colum. L. Rev. 1251 (1967); *Cf. Case Note,* 88 Harv. L. Rev. 1911 (1975).

417. Comment, *The Local Rules of Civil Procedure in the Federal District Courts—A Survey,* 1966 Duke L.J. 1011, 1013.

418. Rule No. 1 (M.D. Ala., Mch. 7, 1961) 1 Fed. Local Ct. Rules (1972) (Representation by Counsel in Civil Rights Cases).

419. *E.g., Id.,* (M.D. Ala., July 12, 1971) (Rule of Court in Six-Member Juries in Civil Cases).

420. See, *e.g.,* Rule No. 6 (S.D. Tex., July 1, 1972. 2 Fed. Local Ct. Rules (1973) (Class Actions: Solicitations and Communication Forbidden).

421. Rule No. 23 (W.D. Mo.) 1 Fed. Local Ct. Rules (1973) (Establishing Panel of Experts and Procedures for Determination of Mental Competency).

422. Rule No. 101.16 (M.D. Pa., July 6, 1973) 2 Fed. Local Ct. Rules (1973) (Use of Photography, Radio and Television Equipment in the Courtroom and its Environs).

423. *Id.* Rule No. 11A (S.D.N.Y., April 30, 1970 (1970) (Class Actions).

424. *Id.* Rule No. 5 (W.D. Okla., Jan. 1, 1971) (1971) Habeas Corpus). *Cf.* proposed Model Local Rule and Complaint in Social Security and Black Lung Litigation proposed by the Acting General Counsel of the Department of Health, Education and Welfare and circulated to district judges by the Administrative Office of the United States Courts at the request of the Committee on Court Administration of the Judicial Conference "with a recommendation for favorable action." Letter of director to District Judges dated March 1, 1976. There was apparently no independent study by the Committee on Court Administration. Letter to author from deputy director of Administrative Office dated March 11, 1976.

425. See, Weinstein, *Routine Bifurcation of Jury Negligence Trial: An Example of the Questionable Use of Rule Making,* 14 Vand. L. Rev. 831 (1961).

426. Note, *Rule 83 and the Local Federal Rules,* 67 Colum. L. Rev. 1251, 1251-52 (1967). For a further collection of practices regulated by local rules see 12 Wright & Miller, Federal Practice & Procedure: Civil § 3154 (1973).

427. Comment, *The Local Rules of Civil Procedure in the Federal District Courts—A Survey,* 1966 Duke L.J. 1011, n.4 (citations and emphasis omitted). For a collection of cases in which local district court rules were declared invalid and in conflict with Rule 83 see 7 Moore's Federal Practice ¶ 83.03; see also, 43 Fordham L. Rev. 1086, 1096 n.78-79 (1975).

428. The arrangements for public distribution are subject to the approval of the director of Administration of the United States District Courts.

429. Communications from the clerk of the Supreme Court and the Administrative Office to the author indicate that there is a passive filing without any attempt at supervision or analysis.

430. 12 Wright & Miller, Federal Practice & Procedure: Civil, § 3151 n.12 (1973).

431. *See, e.g.,* Fed. Rules Serv. (looseleaf collection of local rules); Federal Bar Council, Second Circuit Redbook (M. White ed. 1975-76).

432. Fed. Rules Serv.

433. But see United States v. Columbia Broadcasting System, Inc., 497 F.2d 102, 103 n.3 (5th Cir. 1974) (not properly promulgated because no copy sent to Supreme Court).

434. 12 Wright & Miller: Civil § 3152, p. 219 (1973).

435. *See, e.g.,* Miner v. Atlass, 363 U.S. 641, 80 S.Ct. 1300, 46 L.Ed.2d 462 (1960) (admiralty depositions); Wingo v. Wedding, 418 U.S. 461, 94 S.Ct. 2842, 41 L.Ed.2d 879 (1974) (delegation to master of responsibility of conducting evidentiary hearing); Rodgers v. United States Steel Corp., 508 F.2d 152 (3d Cir. 1975) (communication with absent class members); Chicago Council of

Lawyers v. Bauer, 522 F.2d 242 (7th Cir. 1975) (no comment rule); Mathews v. Weber, 423 U.S. 261 (1976) (references to magistrate). See also, *e.g.,* McCargo v. Hedrick, 45 L.W. 2284 (4th Cir. 1976) (local rule's requirements of details in pretrial order puts back common law pleading concepts inconsistent with Federal Rules of Civil Procedure, and is invalid).

436. Note, *Rule 83 and the Local Federal Rules,* 67 Colum. L. Rev. 1251, 1263 (1967) ("[O] nly a foolhardy lawyer would, by defying such a rule, invite an unfavorable ruling which might or might not be reversed on appeal.").

437. Mathews v. Weber, 423 U.S. 261, 265 n.2 (1976).

438. 522. F.2d 242 (7th Cir. 1975).

439. *Id.* at 248.

440. *Id.* at 251.

441. *Id.* at 259-60.

442. 226 U.S. 673 (1912).

443. *See* Note, *Rule 83 and the Local Federal Rules,* 67 Colum. L. Rev. 1251, 1265 n.77 (1967).

444. 7 Moore's Federal Practice ¶ 83.02.

445. *Id.* at p. 83-3.

446. See Speedy Trial Act of 1974, 18 U.S.C.A. § 3165(c) (1975) (plan "prepared by" the district court to be submitted to a reviewing panel consisting of the Council of the Circuit—that is, the regular judges of the court of appeals—plus the chief judge of the district whose rules are being reviewed or his designee); Fed. R. Crim. P. 50(b), as amended March 18, 1974, effective July 1, 1974.

447. 514 F. 2d 1098 (2d Cir. 1975).

448. *Id.* at 1105.

449. *Id.* at 1105.

450. *Id.* at 1105.

451. 18 U.S.C.A. §§ 3161-74 (1975). See also the activities in this connection of the Federal Judicial Center, Annual Report, p. 14 (1975). *Cf.* 1975 Annual Report. United States Courts for the Second Circuit 93 (mimeograph).

452. Letter of Chief Judge of the Second Circuit, Irving Kaufman, to the author, October 14, 1975; Resolutions of the Eastern District of New York, October 20, 1975. See also, *e.g.,* letter of Chief Judge of E.D.N.Y., Jacob Mishler, to Chief Judge of Second Circuit suggesting Eastern District Court change to model plan drafted by the Administrative Office, July 31, 1975, and response of August 18, 1975; memorandum of Circuit Executive to Second Circuit judges, August 22, 1975; memorandum of Chief Judge Mishler to Eastern District Judges submitting "Judicial Council Recommended Amendments to Conform Rule 50(b)," September 17, 1975; memorandum of Judge Judd to Chief Judge Mishler, October 6, 1975; memorandum of author to Chief Judge Mishler, October 8, 1975; memorandum of Judge Judd to Eastern District judges, October 17, 1975; letter of Judge Judd to Chief Judge of the Second Circuit, October 20, 1975; memorandum of Judge Judd to the Judicial Council, October 28, 1975. Despite requests that the Judicial Council hear the Eastern District Judges opposing the Second Circuit model, such a hearing was not arranged (Minutes, Regular Meeting, Board of Judges of United States District Court, Eastern District of New York, October 20, 1975) until a compromise was worked out in 1976 in meetings between Judges Judd and Mansfield. The public was not privy to these discussions. See Weinstein, *Reform of Federal Court Rulemaking Procedures,* 76 Colum. L. Rev. 905 at nn. 270-71.

453. See 24 United States Attorneys Bulletin 10 (Jan. 9, 1976) ("Many Speedy Trial Act battles lie ahead," describing cases to date). See also memorandum of Professor Avtam Soifer, Speedy Trial Planning Committee Reporter, to Judges of District of Conn., 3 (March, 1976) ("There is a split between the Justice Department and the Administrative Office on the question of the applicability of Section 3161(h) excludable time periods to the Section 3164 interim 90-day time limits."); Telex to all U.S. Attorneys from H. M. Ray, chairman, Legislative and Court Rules Subcommittee, Attorney General's Advisory Committee of United States Attorneys (October 20, 1975).

454. See the letter of February 12, 1976, from the "Speedy Trial Coordinator" of the Administrative Office of the United States Courts, listing the following:

Notes

Issuance Number	Type of item and Subject	Persons to whom sent
1* (9/17/75)	*Speedy Trial Directive* Revised Criminal Docketing and Criminal Statistics Reporting System	Chief District Court Judges, Full Time U.S. Magistrates, Circuit Executives, Public Defenders, Clerks of Court and Deputy Clerks in Charge of Divisional Offices
2 (11/14/75)	*Speedy Trial Advisory* Clarification of certain docketing and statistical reporting procedures	All District Court Clerks
3 (11/21/75	*Speedy Trial Advisory* Ninth Circuit Court of Appeals Decision regarding applicability of "interim limits" in case of U.S. vs. Sara Jane Moore	All Federal Judges, U.S. Magistrates, Federal Public Defenders, Planning Group Reporters, and Clerks of Court
4 (12/5/75)	*Speedy Trial Advisory* Time from Filing to Trial for defendants terminated in 1974	Members of Speedy Trial Planning Groups
5 (12/5/75)	*Speedy Trial Advisory* Availability of Speedy Trial Conference audio cassettes	Members of Speedy Trial Planning Groups
6 (5/19/75)	*Speedy Trial Advisory* Alternative procedures for inter-district notification of defendants arrests	District Court Clerks, U.S. Magistrates, Members of Speedy Trial Planning Groups
7 (12/31/75)	*Speedy Trial Directive* System for Tracking Pretrial Service Agency (PSA) Program Evaluation Data	Chief U.S. Probation Officers, Chief Pretrial Service Officers, Probation Officers in Charge of Units

200

8 (1/13/76)	*Speedy Trial Directive* Request for copies of district or Appeals Court interpretive opinions bearing on the Act	Clerks of District Courts, and Members of Speedy Trial Planning Groups
9 (1/16/76)	*Speedy Trial Advisory* Recommended Outline for district plans under the Speedy Trial Act	Members of Planning Groups, Chief Circuit Judges, and Circuit Executives
10 (2/11/76)	*Speedy Trial Advisory* District Court decision in U.S. vs. Soliah, interpreting "Interim Time limits" under 18 U.S.C. § 3164	All Federal Judges, Members of Planning Groups, and Circuit Executives
11 (2/76)	*Speedy Trial Advisory* Recommended model district plan statement of time limits and procedures for achieving prompt disposition of criminal cases	Members of Planning Groups, Chief Circuit Judges, and Circuit Executives
12 (3/30/76)	*Speedy Trial Advisory* Decision in *U.S.* v. *Tirasso,* interpreting "interim" time limits under 18 U.S.C. § 3164.	All Federal Judges, Planning Group Members, and Circuit Executives

*This was initially released without an issuance number.

On January 31, 1977, the 19th bulletin on this subject was issued bringing to the attention of the courts United States v. Corley, No. 76-2096 (D.C. Cir., December 28, 1976).

455. Standards for Practice by Attorneys (2d Cir. 1975) N.Y. Fed. Ct. Rules 4-13.1.

456. See Weinstein, *Proper and Improper Interactions Between Bench and Law School,* 50 St. Johns L. Rev. 441, 451 n.31 (1976). It is somewhat amusing that the late Professor Bickel who

argued the Pentagon Papers cases in the Second Circuit and Supreme Court, would probably not have qualified for admission in the circuit without some special exemption. See Polsky, *In Praise of Alexander Bickel,* Commentary 52 (Jan. 1976) ("in his twenty-five years . . . in the . . . profession Alexander Bickel had never argued a case in any court, save . . . a small claim in New Haven. . . .").

457. See, *e.g.,* Weinstein, *Questionable Proposals to Make Admission to the Federal Bar More Difficult,* 6 ALI-ABA CLE Review (Dec. 5, Dec. 12, Dec. 19, 1975); Ehrlich, *A Critique of the Proposed New Admission Rule for District Courts in the Second Circuit,* 61 A.B.A.J. 1385 (1975); statement of Dean Michael Sovern of the Columbia Law School at public hearings held November 20, 1974, at Association of the Bar of the City of New York (unpublished), printed in another form at 67 F.R.D. 577 (1975). The appropriate committees of the Association of the Bar of the City of New York, the County Lawyers' Association, and the Federal Bar Council opposed the proposals. See, *e.g.,* Joint report on the Proposed Rule for Admission to Practice Before the United States District Courts in the Second Circuit, Special Committee on Professional Education and Admissions and Committee on Federal Courts of the Association of the Bar of the City of New York, Nov. 20, 1975 (mimeograph). The result of this debate was that the District Courts for the Southern and Eastern Districts of New York overwhelmingly rejected the proposals. N.Y.L.J. Dec. 22, 1975, at 1, col. 3; N.Y.L.J. Dec. 16, 1975, at 1, col. 2. Some districts did adopt the rule. See N.Y.L.J. Dec. 24, 1975, at 1, col. 3. A national committee appointed by the Chief Justice is now examining the issue.

458. See Commission on Review of the Federal Court Appellate System: Opinion Writing and Publication 2 (1974); Standards for Publication of Judicial Opinions, FJC Research Series No. 73-2 at 5 (August, 1973); Mildner v. Gulotta, 405 F.Supp. 182, 201 (E.D.N.Y. 1975), *aff'd,* 425 U.S. 901, 96 Sup. Ct. 1489 (1976) (Weinstein, J., dissenting). *See also,* Jacobstein, *Some Reflections on the Control of the Publication of Appellate Court Opinions,* 27 Stan. L. Rev. 791 (1975); "Supreme Court Declines to Review Unpublished Opinions Issue," 8 The Third Branch at 4, November, 1976.

Notes

459. See, *e.g.*, Board of Federal Judicial Center, Recommendations and Report to April, 1972, Meeting of the Judicial Conference of the United States (mimeo.); Subcommittee on Federal Jurisdiction, Report to the Chairman and to the Members of the Cmt. on Court Administration 9-10 (mimeo. 1972) (containing responses from various Courts of Appeals); Administrative Office of United States Courts, Report to the Subcom. of Federal Jurisdiction on the Operation of Circuit Opinion Publication Plans (mimeo. Jan. 7, 1975); Kanner, *The Unpublished Appellate Opinion: Friend or Foe?*, 1973 Cal. St. B. J. 387 (July-Aug.); United States v. Joly, 493 F.2d 672, 675-76 (2d Cir. 1974).

460. Letter to author, January 5, 1976.

461. Memorandum of Steven Flanders to Judge Walter E. Hoffman (December 22, 1975). The memorandum reflected the view of many judges when it noted: "... many proposed rules may be assumed to be likely sources of bar opposition, despite their merit. Apart from natural conservatism among the bar, many rules do impose additional burdens, which lawyers naturally oppose. Perhaps prepublication or hearings would allow the courts to minimize the burdens. Perhaps, also, those procedures might harden bar opposition to rules that are desirable and necessary. Why take the chance?" *Id.*

462. Memorandum of Steven Flanders to Judge Walter E. Hoffman, January 9, 1975: "Stuart Cunningham, the clerk for the Northern District of Illinois, tells me that the court has had a procedure to publish proposed local rules, and solicit responses, for the last several years. In addition, they made vigorous efforts to inform the bar that the court is open to suggested rules changes. These are to be proposed to the clerk, who will submit them to the executive committee. Although they do not have the hearing procedure Judge Weinstein mentioned, they seem to have gone about as far as any court to obtain the views of the bar concerning local rules. However, they are considering abandoning the pre-publication procedure. The response has been so slight that it seems not to be worth the effort or delay."

Letter of H. Stuart Cunningham to author, Jan. 22, 1976:
... We received three letters regarding the proposed criminal rules, one of which was from a law clerk to a judge of our own Court. We received approximately six letters regarding the

proposed bankruptcy rules and two letters on the proposed Chapter 11 bankruptcy rules. As our records indicate that some 5,000 attorneys have filed appearance in this Court in civil cases in the last few years, over 500 attorneys filed at least one bankruptcy case a year in that time and at least 50 private attorneys represent criminal defendants, their response rates were most disappointing. (We could, of course, assume that our rules are flawless and no attorney found it necessary to comment or possible to improve on any of them. Alas, I doubt this is the reason for the lack of response!)

I have been in contact with the Federal Practice Committee of the Chicago Bar Association regarding the matter of proposed revisions to the rules. I have arranged to provide them with drafts of proposed rules so that they can go over them and give us their recommendations. The Committee has been eager to participate in the rule-making process. This may result in the Court abandoning publication of the rules for comment, and relying instead on the response of interested committees of the various bar associations for comments on behalf of the legal profession. . . .

463. See, *e.g.*, letter of Judge Eugene A. Wright, United States Court of Appeals for the Ninth Circuit, to the author dated January 19, 1976:

From my experience in this court and in the state court system, I can tell you that it is always wise to work with a bar committee. Lawyers will accept rules, even those they do not like, if they have had an opportunity to be heard before the court finally adopts them. The Washington Supreme Court learned this years ago and it now gives at least six months' notice to the state bar before adopting any rule changes.

Reprinted by permission of the author.

464. See, *e.g.*, K. Davis, Administrative Law Treatise § § 6.04-6.06 (1958); Friendly, *Some Kind of Hearing*, 123 U. Pa. L. Rev. 1267 (1975); Joseph v. U.S. Civil Service Comm.,–F.2d–, 45 U.S.L.W. (D.C. Cir., January 17, 1977) (failure to comply with notice and comment procedures of section 4 of the Administrative Commission regulation which has the same effect as legislation).

465. 363 U.S. 641, 80 S.Ct. 1300, 4 L.Ed.2d 462 (1960).

466. *Id.* at 650, 80 S.Ct. at 1306.

467. 413 U.S. 149, 93 S.Ct. 2448, 37 L.Ed.2d 555 (1973).

468. 339 U.S. 78, 90 S.Ct. 1893, 26 L.Ed.2d 446 (1970).

469. 1971 United States Judicial Conference Report 5-6, 60.

470. See, *e.g.,* Rule No. 4 (N.D. Ala.) 1 Fed Local Ct. Rules (1975), Rule No. 12a (D. Conn. Oct. 1, 1972) *Id.* (1973), Rule No. 14a (D. Del. Jan 1, 1973) *Id.* (1974), No. 1-17(a) (D.D.C. Aug. 1, 1973) *Id.* (1975), Rule No. 18 (N.D. Fla. June 29, 1972) *Id.* (1974). *See also,* Colgrove v. Battin, 413 U.S. 149, 151 n.1, 93 S.Ct. 2448, 2449, 37 L.Ed.2d 522 (1973).

471. 7 Moore's Federal Practice ¶ 83.03 n.4, p. 83-6.

472. Zeisel & Diamond, *"Convincing Empirical Evidence" on the Six Member Jury,* 41 U. Chi. L. Rev. 281 (1974); Zeisel, . . . *And Then There Were None: The Diminution of the Federal Jury,* 38 U. Chi. L. Rev. 710 (1971).

473. *Cf.* Address of Chief Justice Warren Burger, American Bar Association Convention, Feb. 15, 1976 (mimeo. at 2): "An important development initiated by Chief Judge Edward Devitt of Minnesota was the reduction of the jury in civil cases to six members, and this is now the prevailing practice in 82 of the 94 federal district courts."

474. 508 F.2d 152 (3d Cir. 1975), *noted* at 88 Harv. L. Rev. 1911 (1975).

475. Rule No. 34 (W.D.Pa., Apr. 1, 1973) 2 Fed Local Ct. Rules (1975).

476. 508 F.2d at 162-63.

477. *Id.* at 163.

478. See Chicago Council of Lawyers v. Bauer, 522 F.2d 242 (7th Cir. 1975), where the local rule was stricken as "overbroad." *Cf.* Landau & Roney, *Fair Trial and Free Press: A Due Process Proposal,* 62 A.B.A.J. 55 (1976).

479. See United States v. Furey, 514 F.2d 1098 (2d Cir. 1975), and Hanna v. Plumer, 380 U.S. 460, 85 S.Ct. 1136, 14 L.Ed.2d 8 (1965), discussed above.

Notes

480. *Cf.* Doran v. United States, 475 F.2d 742 (1st Cir. 1973) (United States Attorney not aware of rule; effective means of promulgation and recompilation should be developed).

481. 12 Wright & Miller, Federal Practice and Procedure: Civil § 3152, p. 220 (1973).

482. American Trial Lawyers Ass'n. v. New Jersey Supreme Court, 66 N.J. 258, 330 A.2d 350 (1974). See also American Trial Lawyers Ass'n. v. New Jersey Supreme Court, 409 U.S. 467, 93 S.Ct. 627, 34 L.Ed.2d 651 (1973) (per curiam) (remand to three-judge federal court to await conclusion of state court proceedings). *Cf.* Gair v. Peck, 6 N.Y.2d 97, 188 N.Y.S.2d 491 (1959), *appeal dismissed,* 361 U.S. 374, 80 S.Ct. 401 (1960).

483. American Trial Lawyers Ass'n. v. New Jersey Supreme Court, 66 N.J. 258, 330 A.2d 350, 354 (1974).

484. *Id.*

485. The New York court fixed limitations on contingency fees were adopted after public hearings. See for a discussion, Gair v. Peck, 6 N.Y.2d 97, 188 N.Y.S.2d 491, 160 N.E.2d 43 (1959), *cert. denied* and *appeal dismissed,* 361 U.S. 374, 80 S.Ct. 401, 4 L.Ed.2d 380 (1960). See, *e.g.,* Note, *Appellate Court's Power to Establish Contingent Fee Schedule,* 60 Colum. L. Rev. 242 (1960).

486. 12 Wright & Miller, Federal Practice and Procedure: Civil § 3153, p. 220 (1973).

487. Blair, *The New Local Rules for Federal Practice in Iowa,* 23 Drake L. Rev. 517, 520 (1974).

488. 12 Wright & Miller, Federal Practice and Procedure: Civil, § 3152, p. 223 (1973).

489. *Id.*
It is interesting that after adoption of the Federal Rules of Civil Procedure a committee of district judges appointed by the Judicial Conference did provide a "draft of local rules" based on the new federal practice. The Committee noted that there are few matters that needed to be treated by local rules and that many rules were in conflict with the procedure. See the abridged report to the Judicial Conference of the Committee on Local District Court Rules, 1940, printed in 4 Federal Rules Service 696 (1941). See also the interesting article by Tobin, *The Foreign Subpoena: A*

Notes

Proposal for Improvement, 62 Georgetown L.J. 1531 (1974) (providing a tabulation of the current requirements for obtaining a foreign subpoena under the practice of most of the United States District Court clerks, rehearsing some of the history of national and local rule-making, and proposing a national rule to provide for uniformity with respect to foreign subpoenas). Mr. Tobin, in a letter to the author dated January 10, 1977, suggested that it is time to reconvene a special committee on local court rules using procedures similar to that described in 1 F.R. Service, *supra.*

490. See Comment, *The Local Rules of Civil Procedure in the Federal District Courts—A Survey,* 1966 Duke L.J. 1011. A curious example of "national" local rules" is the proposed "Model Local Rule and Complaint v. Social Security and Black Lung litigation." It was forwarded to all United States district judges by the director of the Administrative Office of the United States Courts by letter dated March 1, 1976, "at the request of the Committee on Court Administration of the Judicial Conference with a recommendation for favorable action." Apparently it was first sent to the Administrative Office by letter dated January 7, 1976, from the Office of General Counsel of the Department of Health, Education and Welfare with a letter indicating that it had been drafted by the General Counsel's office and the Department of Justice. There is no indication of publication in advance—as probably would have been required had an administrative regulation been adopted. Nor is any explanation given why, if a uniform national rule was required, the ordinary national rule-making procedures of amending the Federal Rules of Civil Procedure should not have been followed.

491. 363 U.S. 641, 649-50, 80 S.Ct. 1300, 1305-6, 4 L.Ed.2d 462 (1960).

492. Adm. R. 30A, 368 U.S. 1023 (1961).

493. Fed. R. Crim. P. 29.1.

494. See the authorities collected in Note, *Rule 83 and the Local Federal Rules,* 67 Colum. L. Rev. 1251, 1255-59 (1967); 12 Wright & Miller, Federal Practice and Procedure: Civil, § 3154, p. 228 (1973); Blair, *The New Local Rules for Federal Practice in Iowa,* 23 Drake L. Rev. 517, 519-520 (1974).

495. Quoted in Note, *Rule 83 and the Local Federal Rules,* 67 Colum. L. Rev. 1251, 1259 (1967).

207

Notes

496. 12 Wright & Miller, Federal Practice and Procedure: Civil § 3152, p. 218 (1973). See the earlier suggestion of uniform district court rules in Judicial Conference Report 1939, p. 7; P. Fish, The Politics of Federal Judicial Administration 149, 348 (1973).

497. P. Fish, The Politics of Federal Judicial Administration 71-74 (1973).

498. See letter from Chief Judge of Second Circuit to Judge Bonsal, November 13, 1975 (cutbacks established by guidelines for payment of attorneys can be waived in an exceptional case, but no such case has arisen). *Cf.* Report of the Proceedings of the Judicial Conference of the United States, September, 1975, p. 75 ("guideline" on payment to the Clerk of court where person's resources and income are sufficient to pay for part of cost of appointed counsel). The Second Circuit guidelines were published *after* adoption. N.Y.L.J. p. 1, July 3, 1973.

499. See letter from George Vician, Jr., Supervising Attorney, Brooklyn Citizenship Section, to Chief Judge Jacob Mishler of the Eastern District of New York, December 23, 1975, requesting a decision by all the judges of the court to avoid the necessity of proof in certain cases involving claims of adultery. The letter noted: "Last year the Judges of the United States District Court, Southern District of New York, as set forth in the letter of the Chief Judge, dated December 27, 1974,' . . . agreed to waive the presentation of a long written report of the results of an outside investigation, together with the Findings of Fact and Conclusions of Law . . . where the adultery during the statutory period for good moral character has been cured by a subsequent marriage. . . ."

500. See, *e.g.*, Feb. 5, 1975, limited stays in criminal appeals; Jan. 31, 1974, use of split trials "whenever possible"; April 4, 1974, avoid referrals of custody disputes to Family Court. *Cf.* also, *i.e.*, Amendments to the Rules of the Administrative Board in Judicial Conference of the State of New York, Report of the Administrative Board, 16 Ann. Rep. A-12 ff. (Leg. Doc. No. 90 (1971).

By contrast, the elaborate Standards and Goals published for New York Courts, have the advantage of being knowable by all who may be affected. *See, e.g.,* Report of The Administrative

Notes

Board of The Judicial Conference, 1975, Leg. Doc. No. 90, at 13-21 (1976).

501. For example, in Mathews v. Weber, 96 Sup.Ct. 549 (1976), the Court dealt with General Order No. 104-D of the Central District of California covering references to magistrates in administrative review matters. This order might well affect an attorney's trial tactics. Yet, an examination of the current Federal Rules Service purporting to contain all current local rules does not reveal this order.

502. See Joint Committee of the Association, The New York County Lawyers' Association, and the Federal Bar Council, *Federal Sentencing Practices*, 30 Record of N.Y.C.B.A. 652 (1975).

In a letter to the author dated February 5, 1977, Judge Suttle of the United States District Court for the Western District of Texas suggests that under some circumstances "standing orders" have the same effect as local rules, although the bar may not receive notice of such standing order. On January 24, 1974, Judge Suttle dissented from an "Amended Order Interpreting Local Court Rule 10." The interpretation apparently dealt with the interest of counsel in bail bond money and the method of refund, individually or jointly, to the lawyer in the case. In a concurring memorandum Chief Judge Spears suggested that it may be "valid" to require all local rules to be adopted only after adequate notice. Cf. Nolan v. The Judicial Council, 481 F. 2d 41, 46-47 (3d Cir. 1973).

503. By resolution of the Board of Judges of the Eastern District of New York, adopted February 9, 1976, those portions dealing with treatment of the presentence report were adopted (without public notice) and embodied in notices of sentencing to be mailed by the probation department. The Second Circuit Judicial Council has recommended adoption of its sentencing guidelines as district rules. See New York Times, March 18, 1976, p. 37, col. 3. The proposed rules are set out in the New York Law Journal, March 18, 1976, p. 1, col. 3. The Sentencing Committee of the Judicial Council of the Second Circuit made an admirable attempt to engage the bar and bench in its deliberations. See letter of Judge Murray I. Gurfein, March 21, 1977, to the author.

504. Rule 25.2 of the General Rules for the Southern and Eastern Districts of New York, amended September 22, 1975 (Weinstein, J., dissenting).

Notes

505. Memorandum to all United States District Judges, Nov. 24, 1975.

506. *Hearings on the Independence of Federal Judges Before the Subcomm. on Separation of Powers of the Senate Comm. on the Judiciary,* 91st Cong., 2d Sess. (1971).

507. See, J. Oliver, *Reflections on the History of Circuit Judicial Councils and Circuit Judicial Conferences,* 64 F.R.D. 201 (1975). *Cf.* Draft Controller General's Report to Congress, "Further Improvements Needed in the Administrative and Financial Operations of the United States District Courts (circulated March 17, 1976), suggesting a stronger administrative role for Judicial Councils in supervising district judges.

508. Chandler v. Judicial Council, 498 U.S. 74, 141, 90 S.Ct. 1648, 1682, 26 L.Ed.2d 100 (1970) (Douglas, J., dissenting); J. Oliver, *Reflections on the History of Circuit Judicial Councils and Circuit Judicial Conferences,* 64 F.R.D. 201, 202 (1975).

509. H.R. Rep. No. 702, 76th Cong., 1st Sess. 2 (1939), *cited* in Chandler v. Judicial Councils 398 U.S. 74, 97, 90 S.Ct. 1648, 1660, 26 L.Ed.2d 100 (1970).

510. 28 U.S.C. § 620 (1970).

511. Letter from Judge Ruggero J. Aldisert to United States Judges, Circuit Court Executives, and Clerks of Court, Jan. 30, 1976.

By contrast, the memorandum of the deputy director of the Administrative Office of the United States Courts, dated January 13, 1976, indicated that the "Addendum to Guidelines to the Amendments to the Federal Rules of Criminal Procedure Which Relate to the Preparation and Use of Presentence Reports" would only be sent to "United States District Judges, Magistrates, Clerks of Court, Public Defenders, and Probation Officers."

512. "The report was prepared in loose leaf form to facilitate changes and additions. This format also permits the inclusion of the report in a benchbook, thus enhancing its utility as a reference tool." Letter from Judge Ruggero J. Aldisert to United States Judges, Circuit Court Executives and Clerks of Court, Jan. 30, 1976.

513. Manual for Complex and Multidistrict Litigation iii-xiii (1970), prepared by a subcommittee of the Co-ordinating Com-

mittee for Multiple Litigation with the assistance of various committees and individuals from the bench, bar, and law schools. *Id.* at viii.

514. See discussion of Rodgers v. United States Steel Corp., *supra* at n. 474.

515. Roney, *The Bar Answers The Challenge,* 62 A.B.A.J. 60, 64 (1976). Reprinted by permission.

516. Blair, *The New Local Rules for Federal Practice in Iowa,* 23 Drake L. Rev. 517, 518 n.6 (1974).

517. Committee on the Federal Courts, The Association of the Bar of the City of New York, Report Evaluating the Individual Assignment System in the Southern District of New York After Three Years Experience July 8, 1975, at 5 (mimeograph) (cited hereafter as Report Evaluating Individual Assignment System). See also Finley v. Parvin/Dohrmann Co., 520 F.2d 386, 389 n.3, 390 (2d Cir. 1875).

518. See also memorandum of Steven Flanders to Judge Walter Hoffman (December 22, 1975): "The objections [to local rule-making] that I think are most significant are the ones that concern procedures of individual judges that are in conflict with local rules, or that modify them so much that the corresponding local rule is meaningless. Examples of the former are rules like those . . . that require papers to be submitted in a form different from that described in a local rule. An example of the latter is the widely different requirements for speed and completeness of pre-trial preparation within the district courts both in Philadelphia and in Los Angeles."

519. Report Evaluating Individual Assignment System at 6.

520. The report, *id.* at 40-41, notes "[t]en judges require . . . papers to be filed only in the Clerk's Office;" one requires that all papers be filed in his office only and six require one set to be filed with the Clerk and another with the judge; ten judges specify that oral argument will only be permitted if the judge considers it appropriate; three require it on all motions; three permit it on request of counsel, and six say nothing about oral argument; and two judges follow the state practice of requiring a Note of Issue or Statement of Readiness in civil cases.

521. *See, e.g.*, testimony of Herbert Semmel on behalf of the National Association of Criminal Lawyers and the Center for Law and Social Policy, *Hearings on Amendments to Federal Rules of Criminal Procedure Before the Subcomm. on Criminal Justice of the House Comm. on the Judiciary*, 94th Cong., 1st Sess., ser. 6, at 168 (1975): "it's quite proper that . . . Congress has finally begun to take a close look at the rules promulgated by the Supreme Court. . . . [I] t's also clear that if Congress undertakes to rewrite every rule change . . . , the rulemaking process is going to be completely undermined. . . ."

522. *See* G. Hazard, Jr., Representation in Rule-making, in Law and the American Future 98 (M.L. Schwartz ed. 1976) ("appointed rule-makers [should] . . . give . . . reasons").

523. B. Schwartz and H. Wade, Legal Control of Government 87 (1972) (referring to the Administrative Procedure Act).

524. *Cf.* Murphy, *Old Maxims Never Die: The "Plain-Meaning Rule" and Statutory Interpretation in the "Modern" Federal Courts*, 75 Colum. L. Rev. 1299 (1975). Without the necessary legislative history, normal federal techniques of interpreting statutes or rules is impossible.

525. See S.A. Scheingold, The Politics of Rights, 33-34 (1974) ("The political appeal and ostensible vitality of legal processes is in part explained by their public and rational character. The courtrooms of the nation are open; the rules that focus litigation are a matter of public record; the judgments that emerge are generally available; they are proceeded by the careful argumentation of the adversary process and are accompanied by a reasoned defense of the decision. If cameras are excluded from the halls of justice and the seating capacity restricted, it is, we are told, in the service of decorum—that is, to create an atmosphere in which reason will prevail—not for purposes of secrecy."). But see J. B. Weinstein, Let the People Observe Their Courts, N.Y.L.J., March 31, 1977, p. 1, col. 1; April 1, 1977, p. 1. col. 2.

526. 28 U.S.C. § 331 (1970).

INDEX

213

Index

214

Index

Law schools, 19, 32
Legal Services Corporation, 113, 149
Legislature v. Courts, 54
Lesnick, Howard, 87
Levin, Leo, 87
Livingston, Robert, 34
Local rules, 4, 11, 117 ff.; appellate supervision, 123; appeals, 121; filing, 120; improvement, 133, 150; kinds, 118 ff.
Los Angeles, 129
Louisiana, 83
Lumbard, Joseph E., 102
Lynch, Joseph M., 82

McClellan, John, 10
Madison, James, 43, 57
Magistrates, xii
Maine, 35
Mapp v. Ohio, 16
Marbury v. Madison, 13, 128
Marshall, John, Chief Justice, 35, 43, 89, 93
Maryland, 35
Mason, George, 43
Massachusetts, 35
Miner v. Atlass, 130, 136
Miranda, 5, 102
Model Code of Evidence, 72
Modification of process, 105 ff.
Monroe, James, 48
Montesquieu, 22, 41
Moore, William, 66, 131
Murphy, Frank, 91
Muskrat v. United States, 49

NAACP Legal Defense Fund, 17, 132

National Legal Aid & Defender Association, 149
New Hampshire, 35
New Jersey, 4, 77 ff., 134
New Mexico, 80
New York, 4, 8, 18, 19, 35, 37, 39, 63, 86, 138, 139, 195
Nixon, Richard M., 78
No-fault statutes, 83-84
North Carolina, 35

Parliament. *See* England; Israel
Parness and Korbakes, 19
Peterson, William, 37
Pennsylvania, 35, 187 n. 331
Philadelphia, 129
Philadelphia Convention, 36
Pinckney, Charles, 37
Plea bargaining, 94
Practicality of process, 76, 77 ff.
Prejudgment interest, 83
Prisoner cases, 141
Privileges, 73, 80, 100, 104
Procedural conservatism, 21
Process acts, 57, 60, 89
Public participation, 7, 74, 106, 129, 152
Publishing opinions, 128

Quasi-rule directives, 137

Radolph, Edmund, 36
Reasons for growth, 12 ff.
Reporter, 86
Rhode Island, 35
Rodgers v. United States Steel Corp., 132
Rome, 162 n. 56
Rosenberg, Maurice, Professor, 137

215

Index

Rosenberg, Samuel, 33
Rules of Decision Act, 65

Schwellenbach, Lewis Baxter, 49
Sentence review, xii
Separation of powers, 36, 53
Sibbach v. Wilson & Co., 90
Sierra Club, 17
South Carolina, 35
South Dakota, 35
Speedy trials, 108, 124 ff.
"Standing," 157 n. 15
Standing Committee, 69, 149
State v. Clemente, 79
Substantive rights affected, 24
Sunderland, E. R., 48
Supremacy clause, 39
Supreme Court of United States, 14, 67, 101 ff.

Taft, William H., 47
Taney, Rogers, Chief Justice, 48
Tate, Albert, Jr., 83
Thomsen, Roszel C., 108

Uniform rules of evidence, 72
United States Judicial Conference, 96, 97, 137
United States v. Fruehauf, 50
United States v. Furey, 125

Vanderbilt, Arthur T., 80, 84
Virginia, 35
Virginia Plan, 37

Warren, Earl, Chief Justice, 9, 50, 72, 104
Washington, George, 47, 78
Wayman v. Southard, 89, 93
Wechsler, Herbert, Professor, 51, 99
Weintraub, Joseph, 81
Wheeler, Burton, 50
Winberry v. Salisbury, 77, 81, 84
Wright, Charles, and Miller, Arthur, 135, 137
Wythe, George, 36, 43
Wyzanski, Charles E., 122

Zeisel, Hans, 131